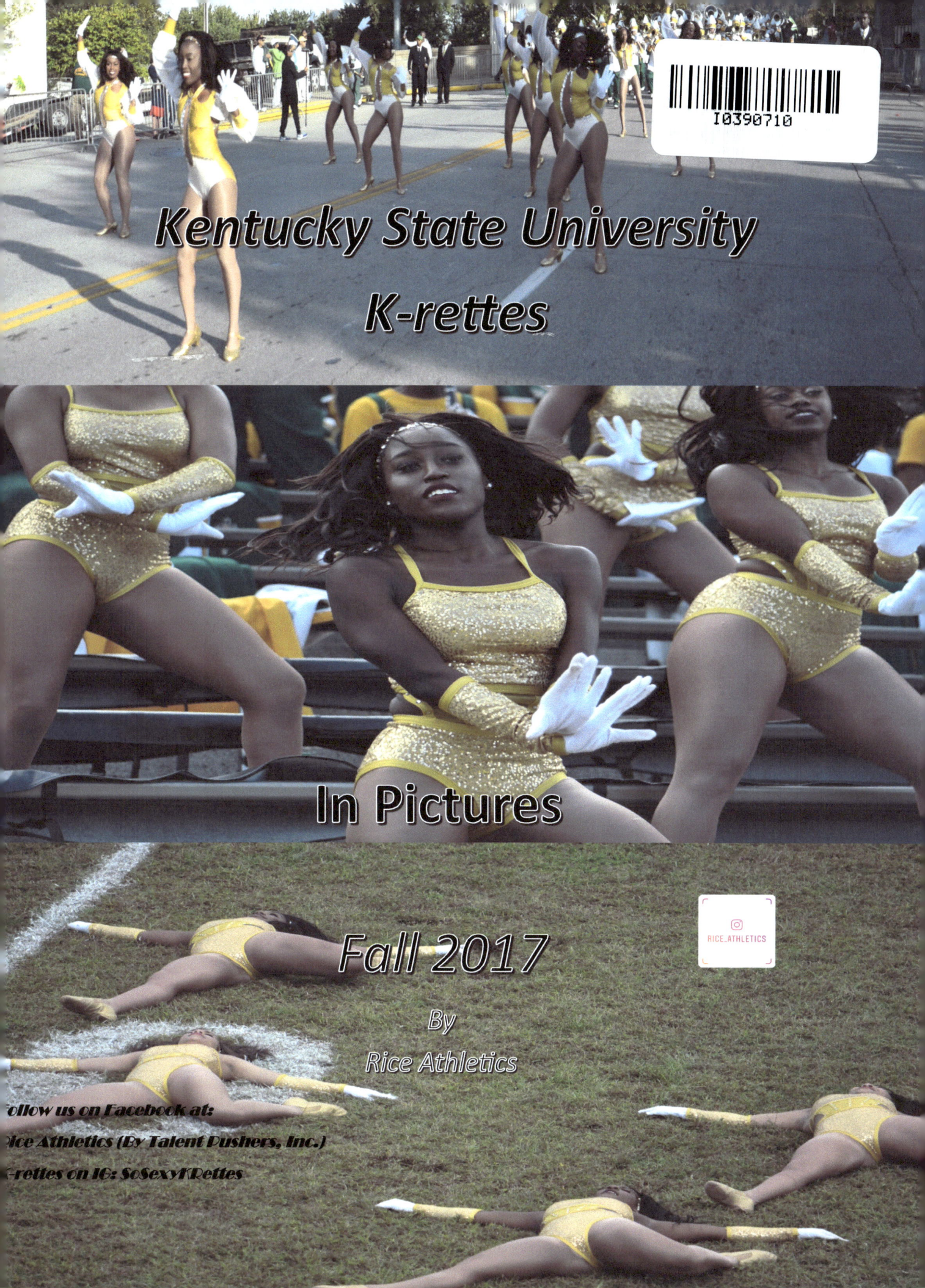

Kentucky State University

K-rettes

In Pictures

Fall 2017

By

Rice Athletics

Follow us on Facebook at:

Rice Athletics (By Talent Pushers, Inc.)

K-rettes on IG: SoSexyKRettes

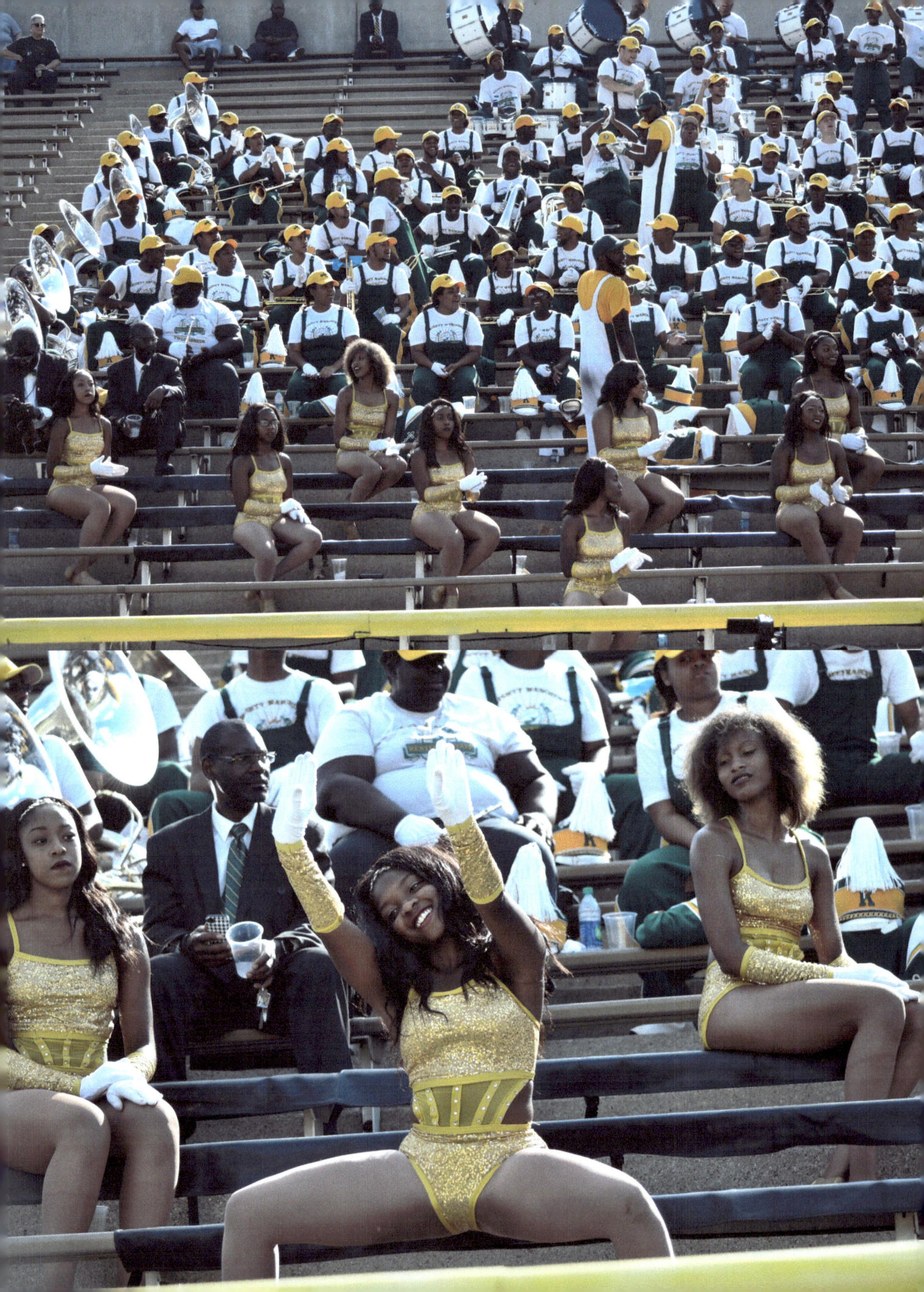

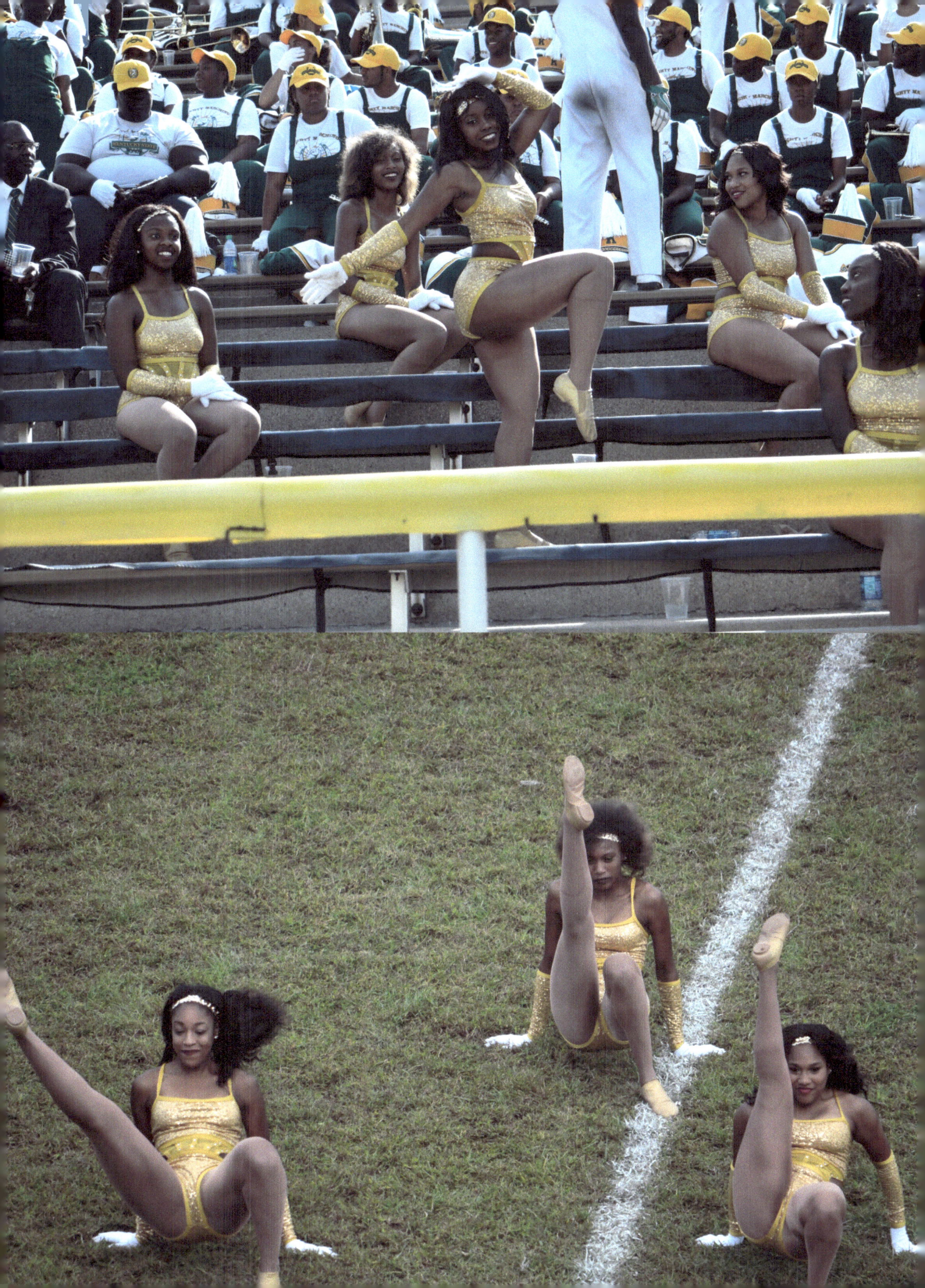

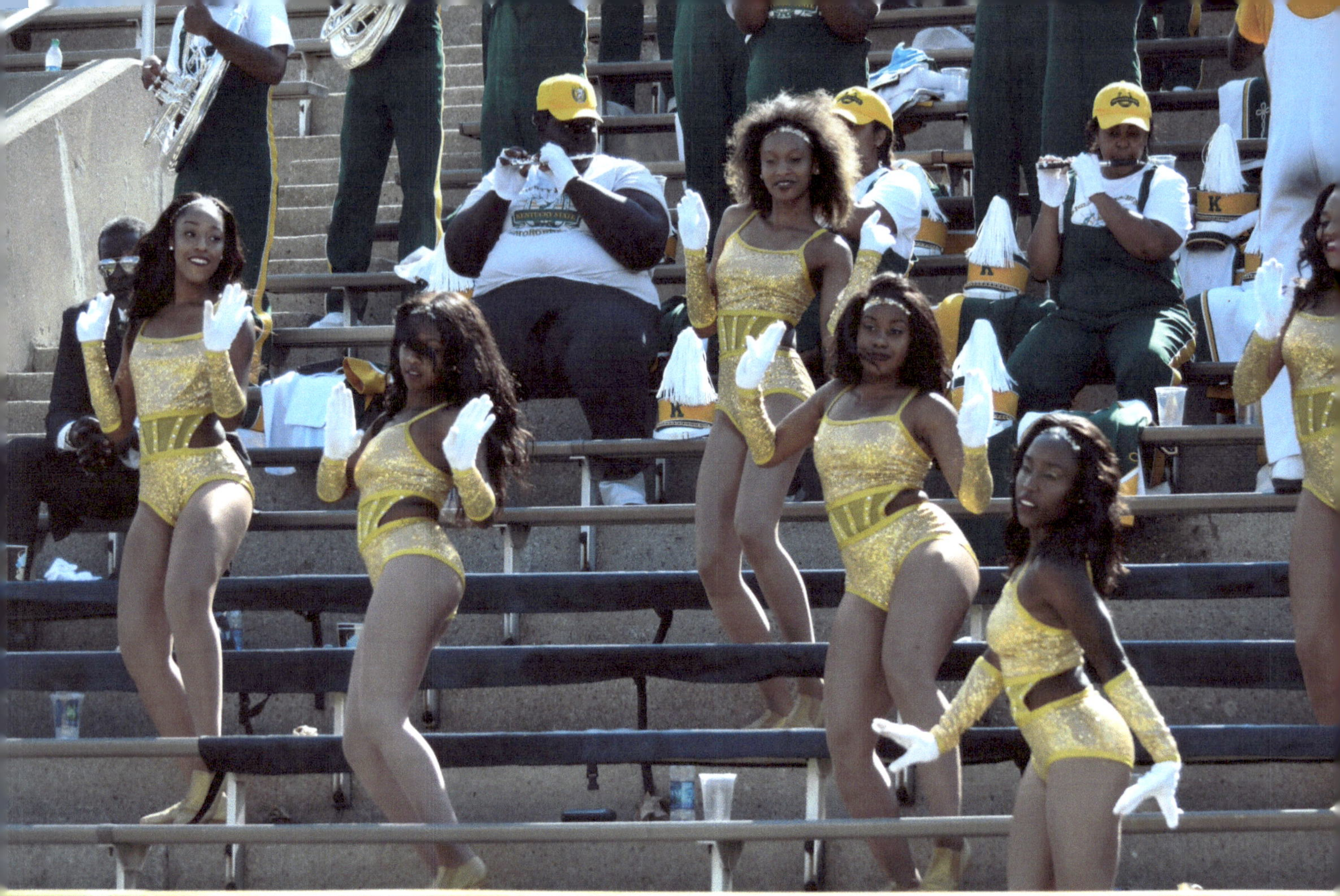

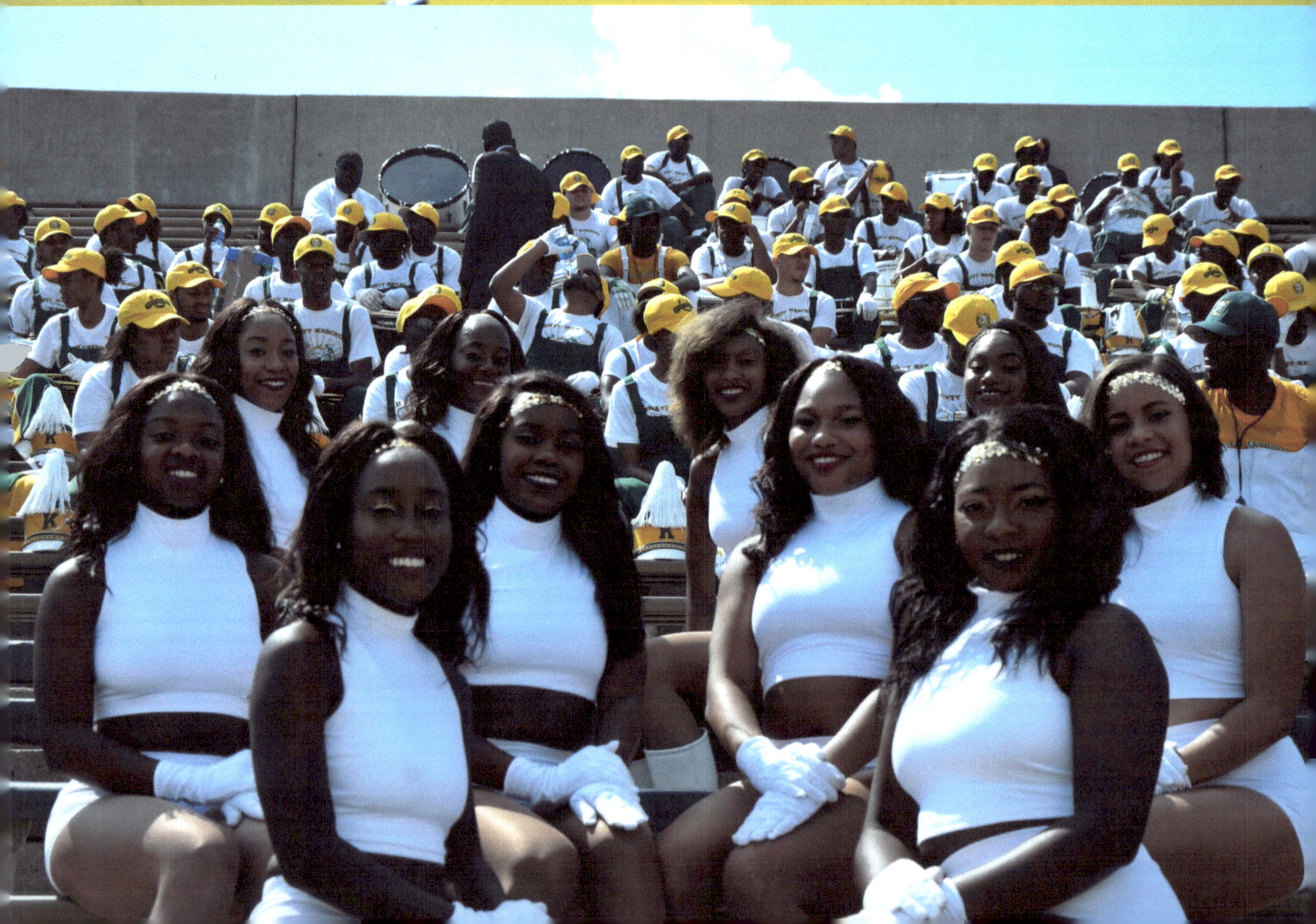

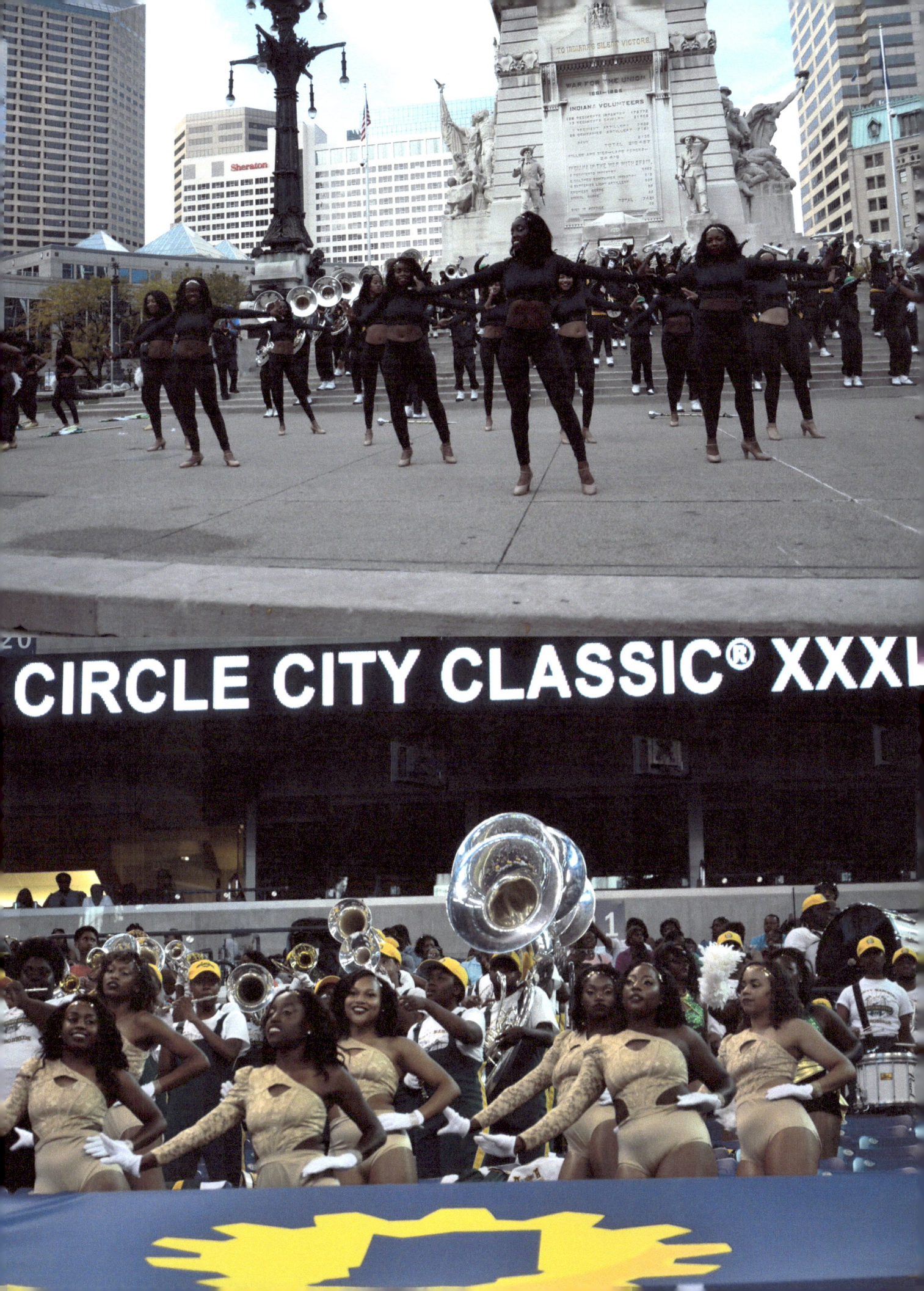

CIRCLE CITY CLASSIC® XXXL

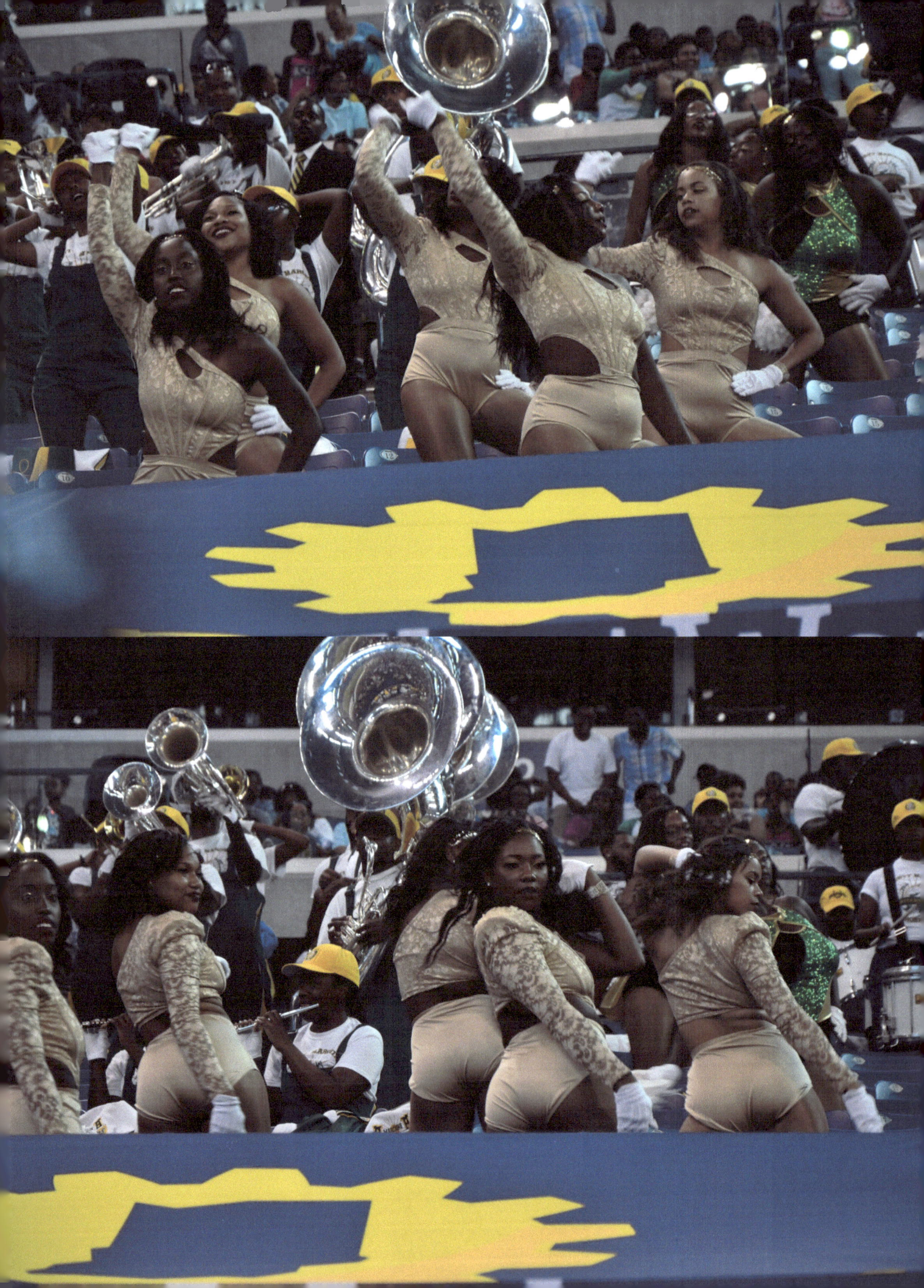

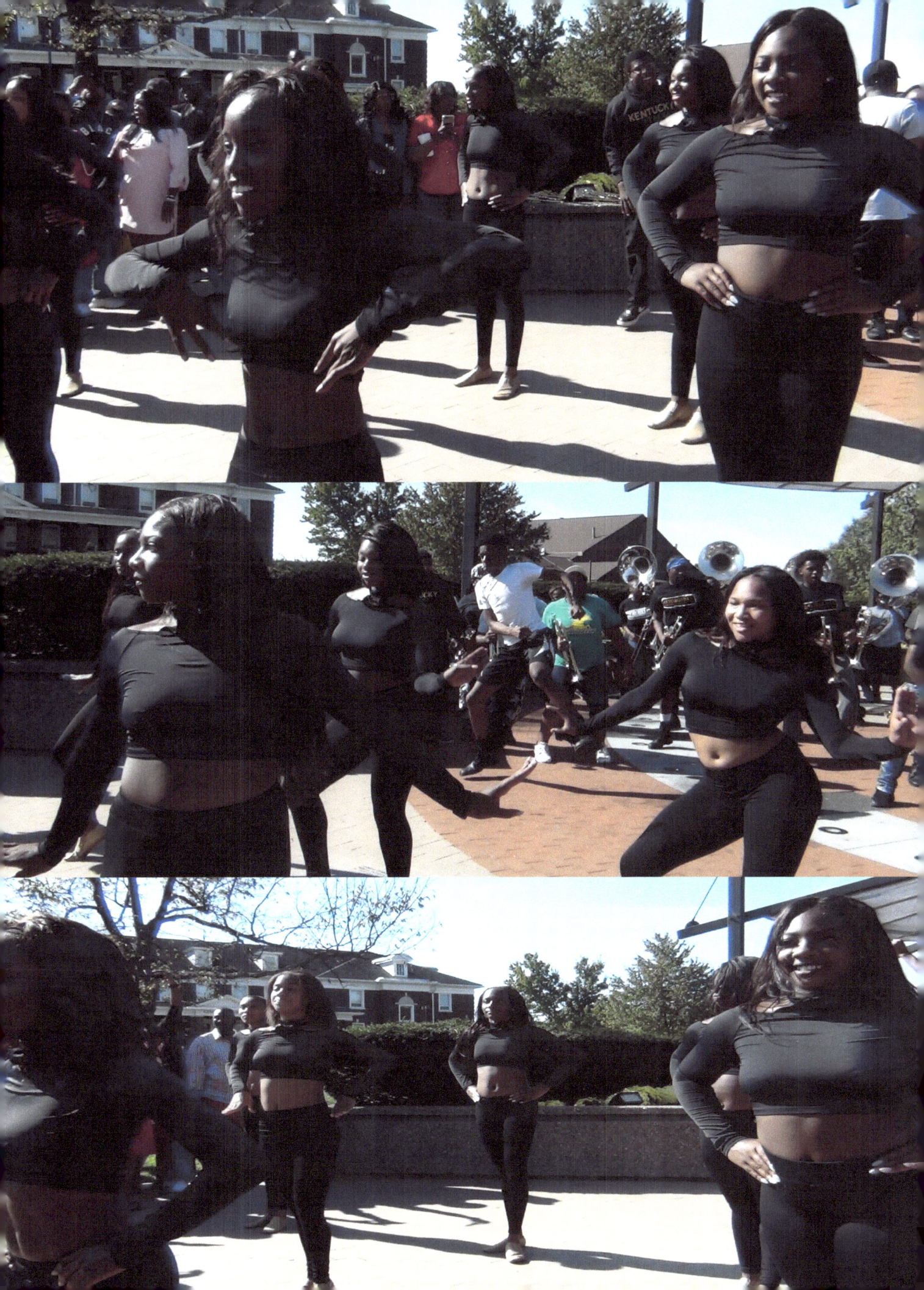

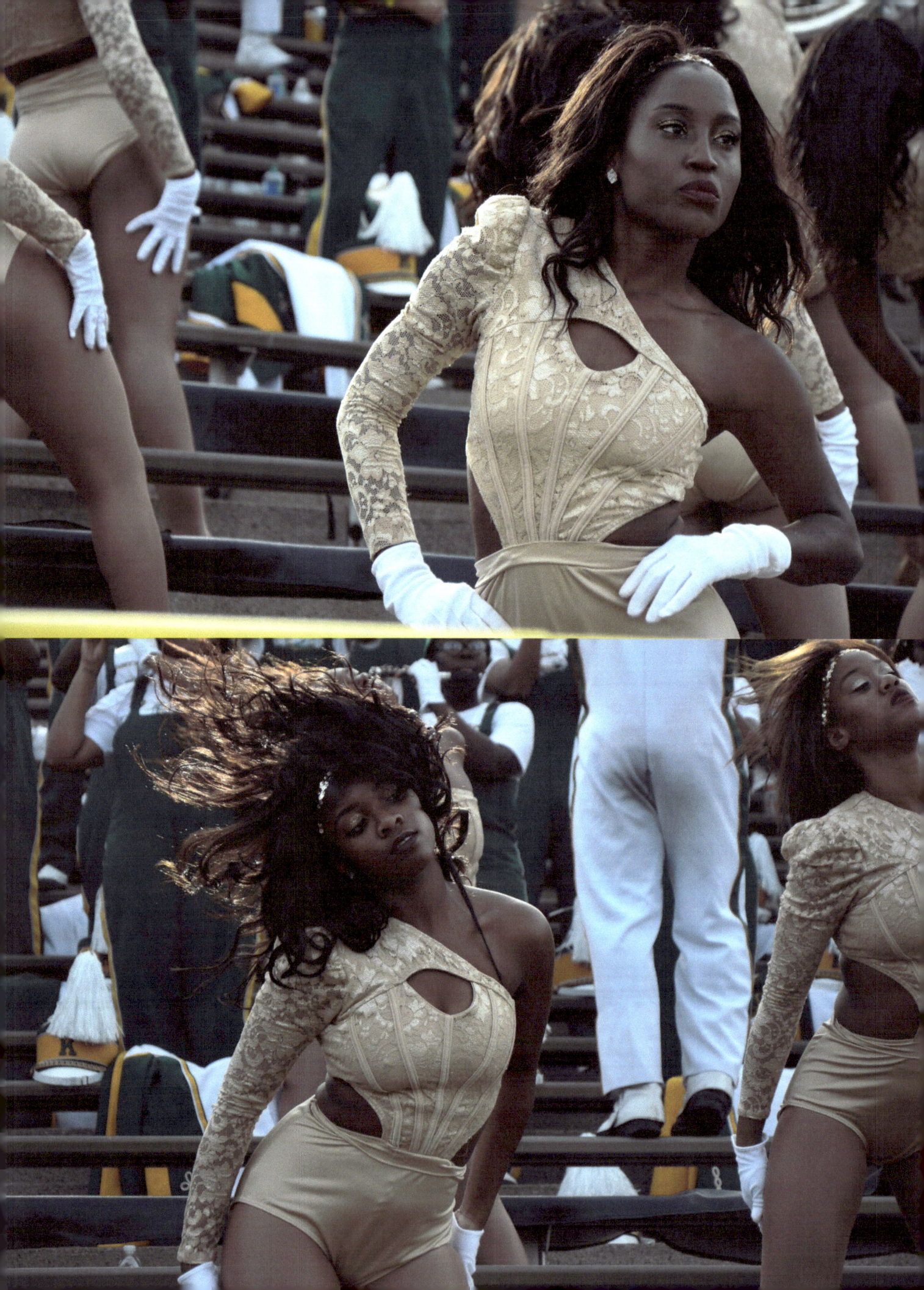

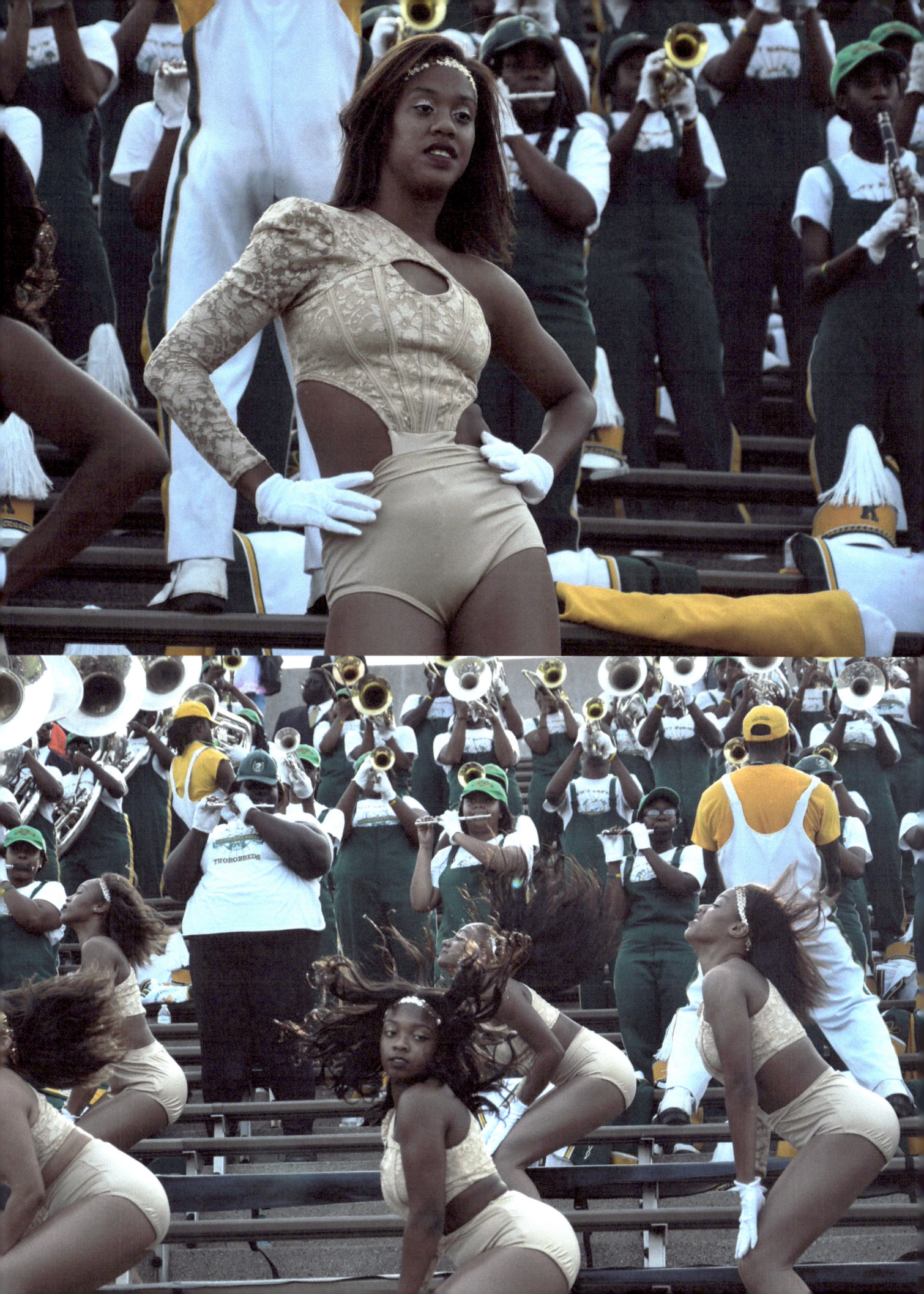

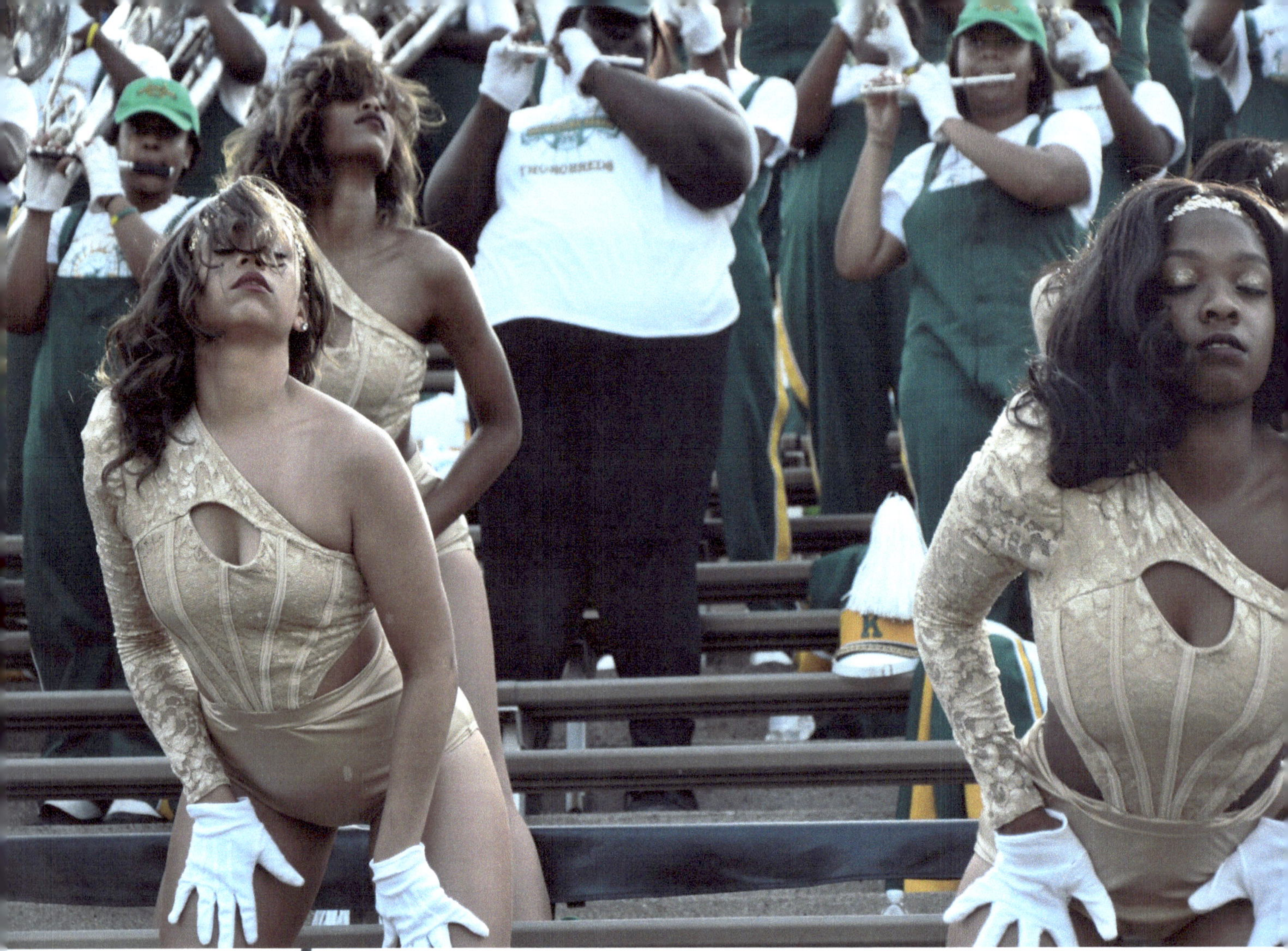

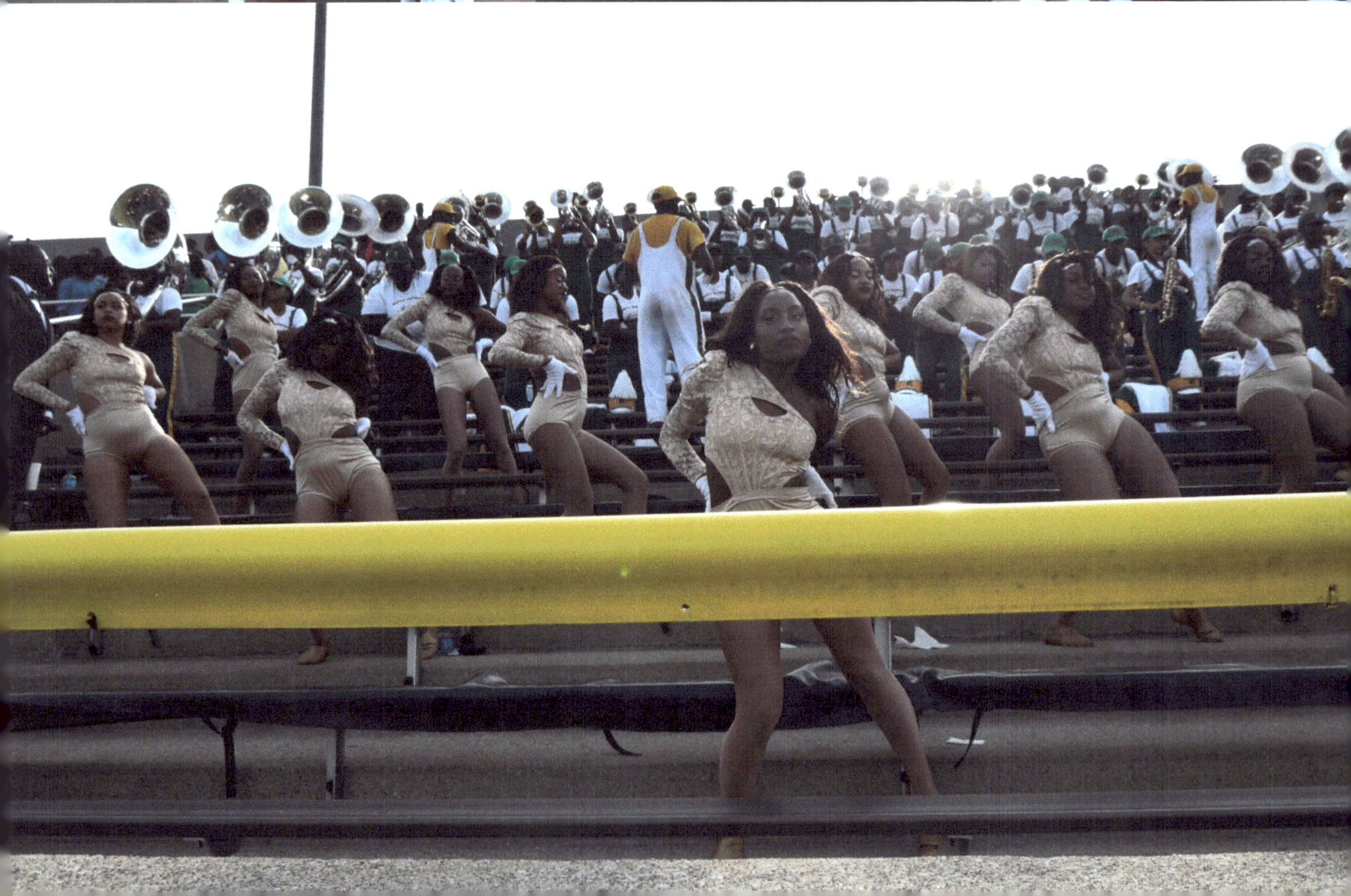

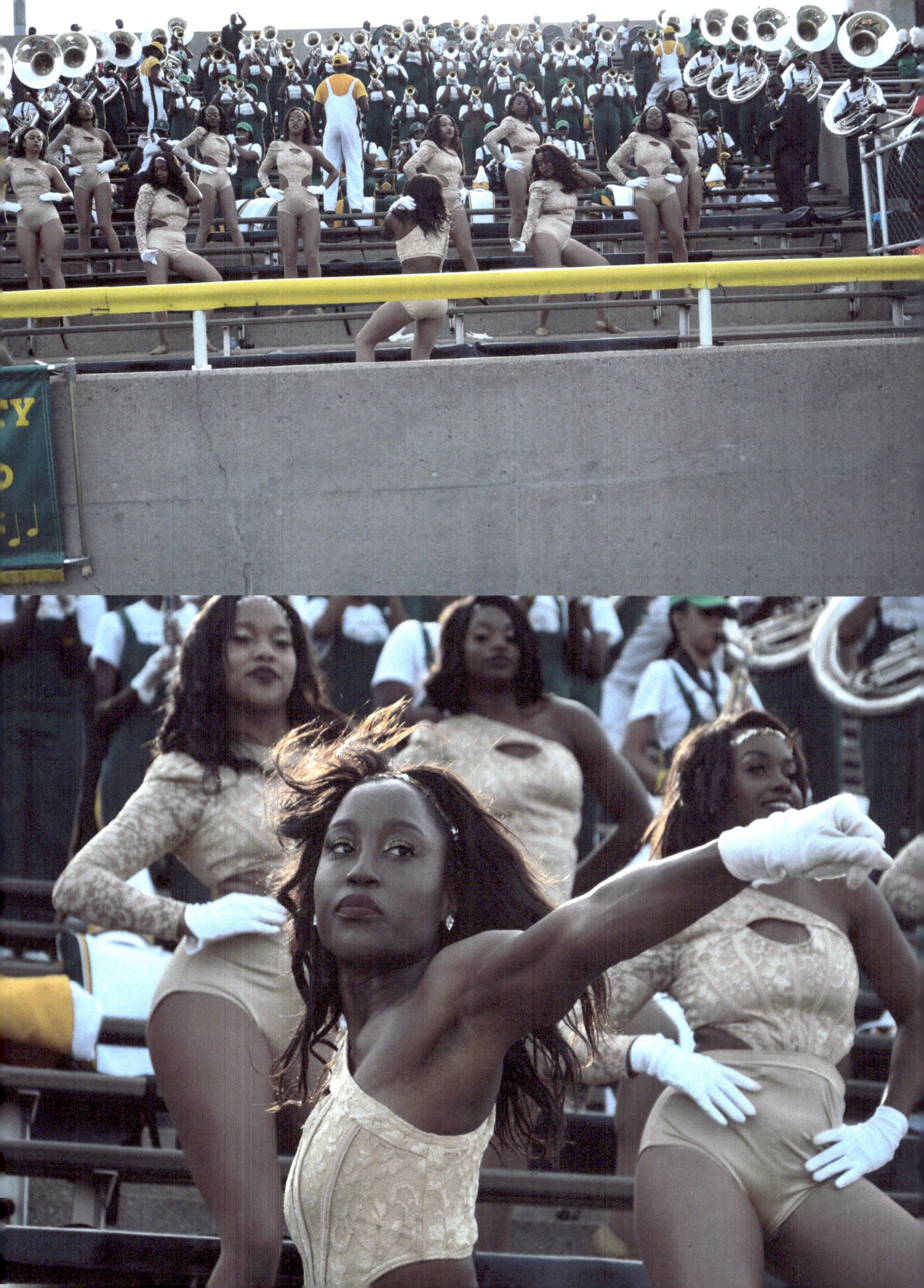

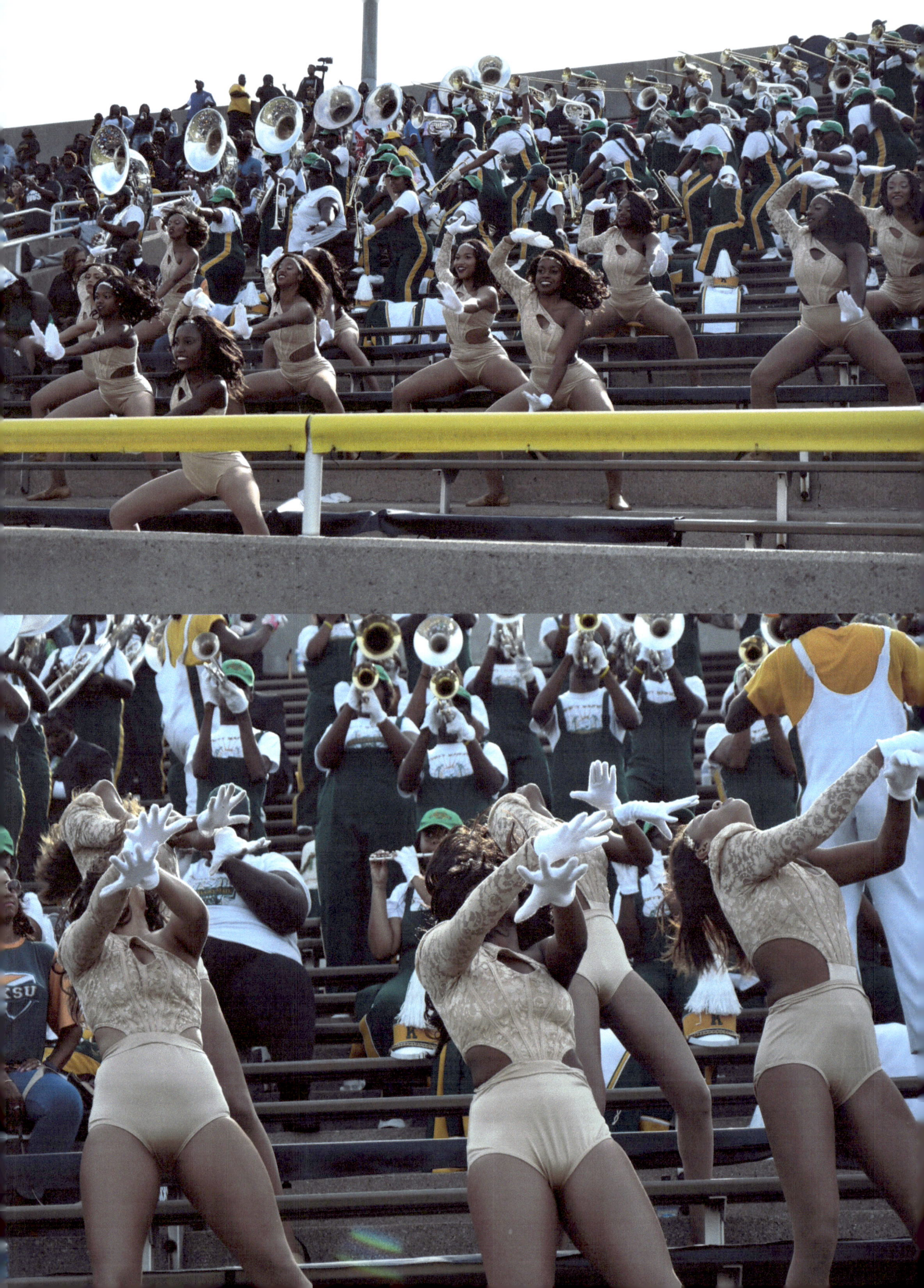

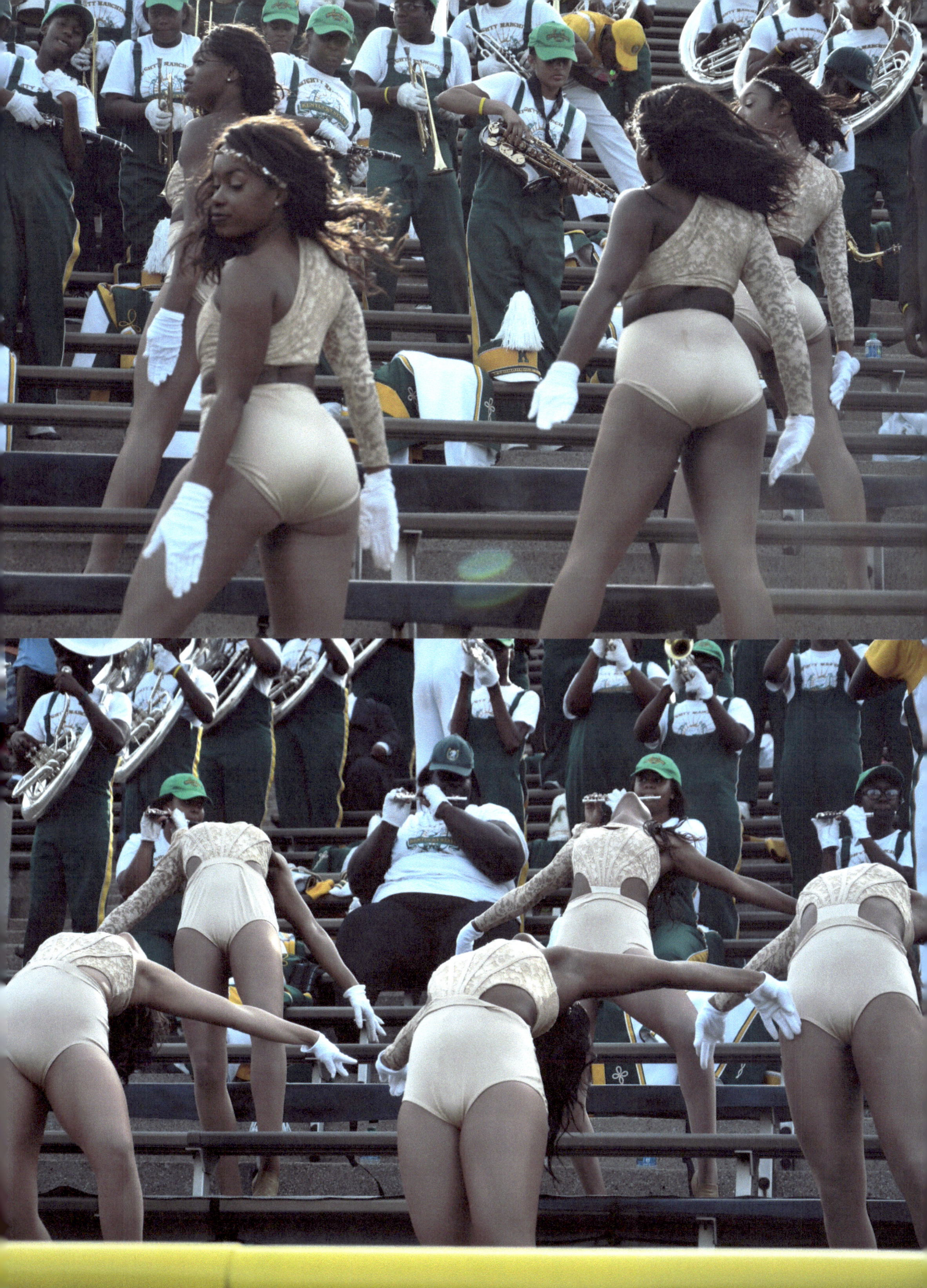

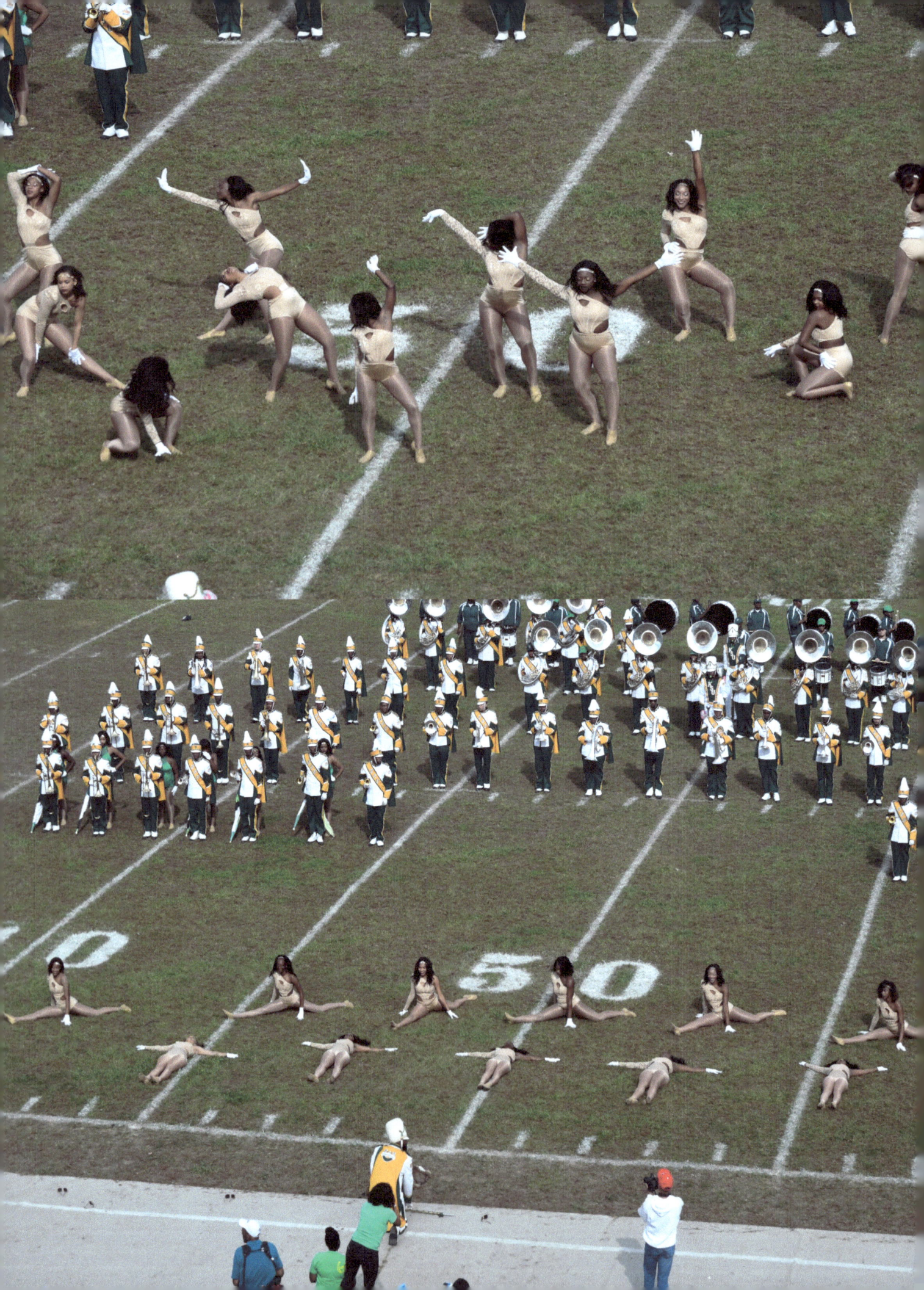

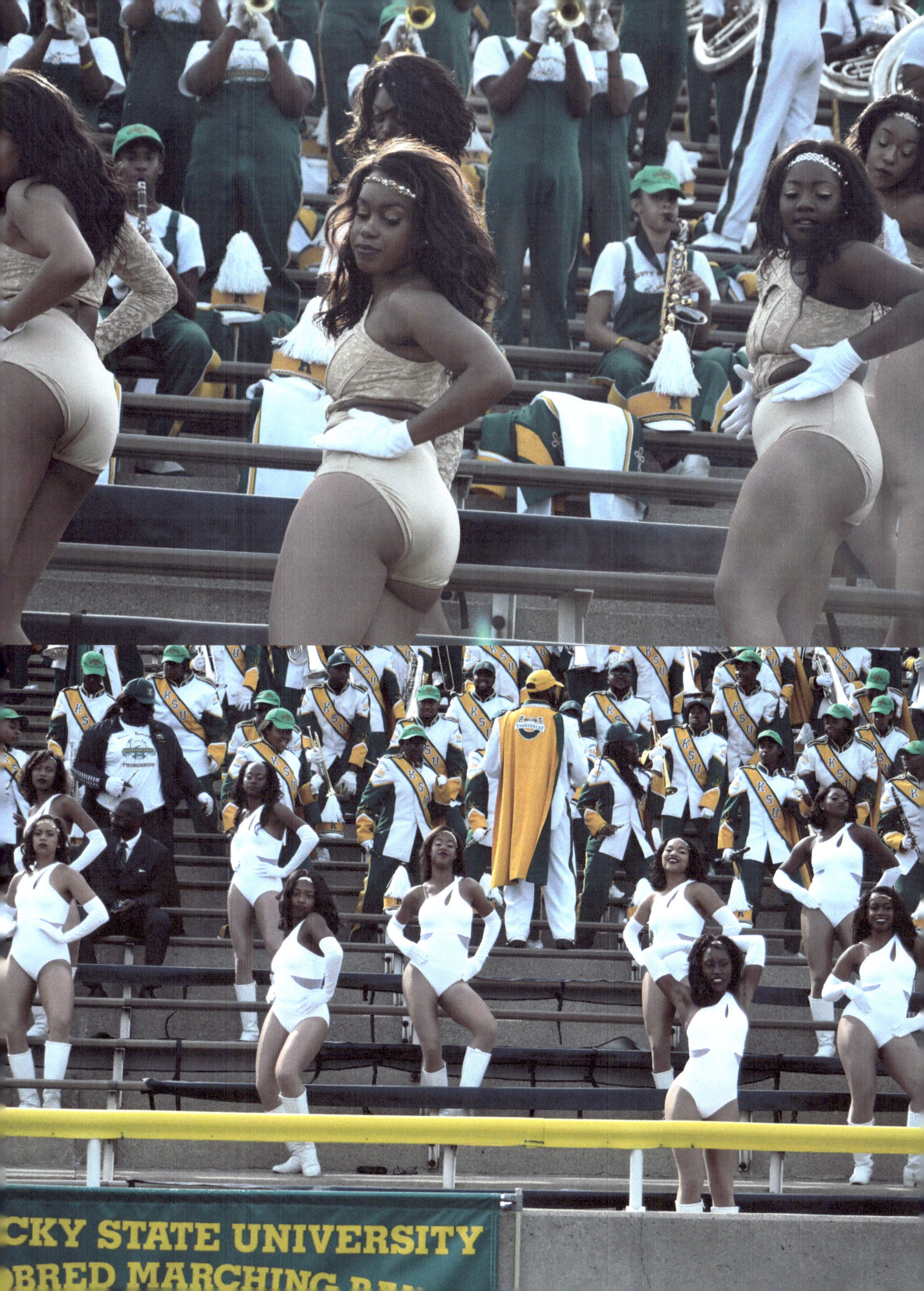

CKY STATE UNIVERSITY
BRED MARCHING BA

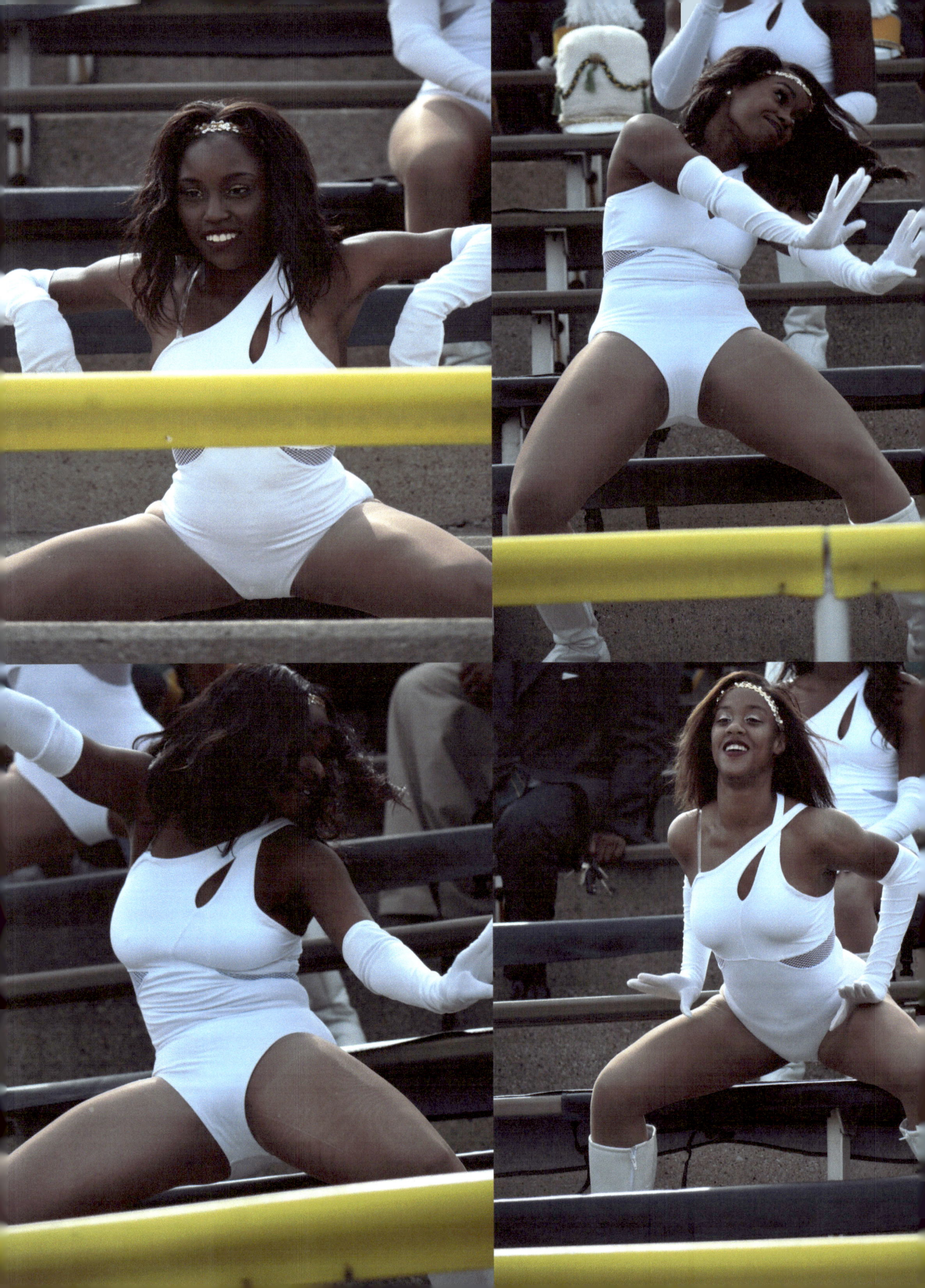

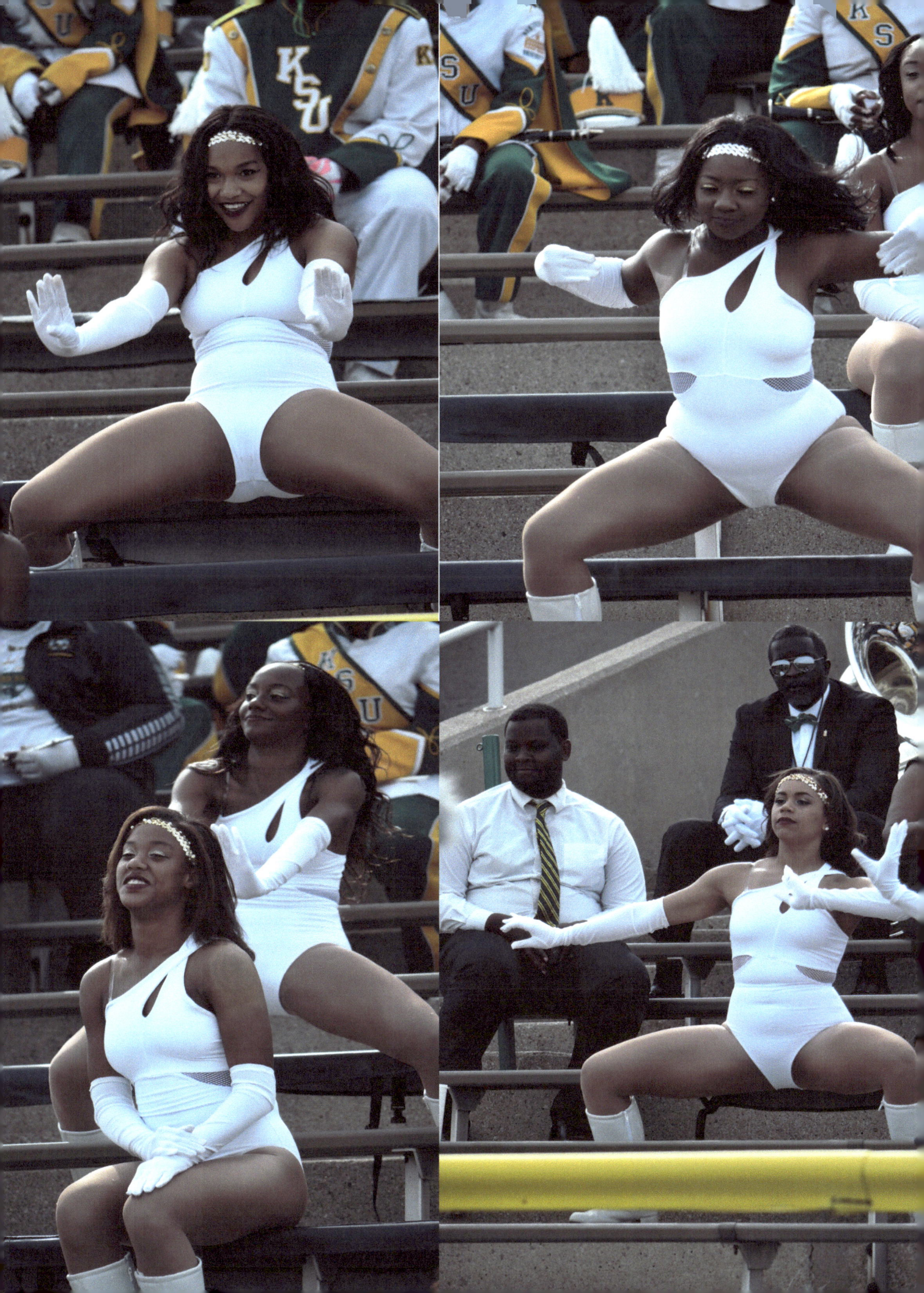

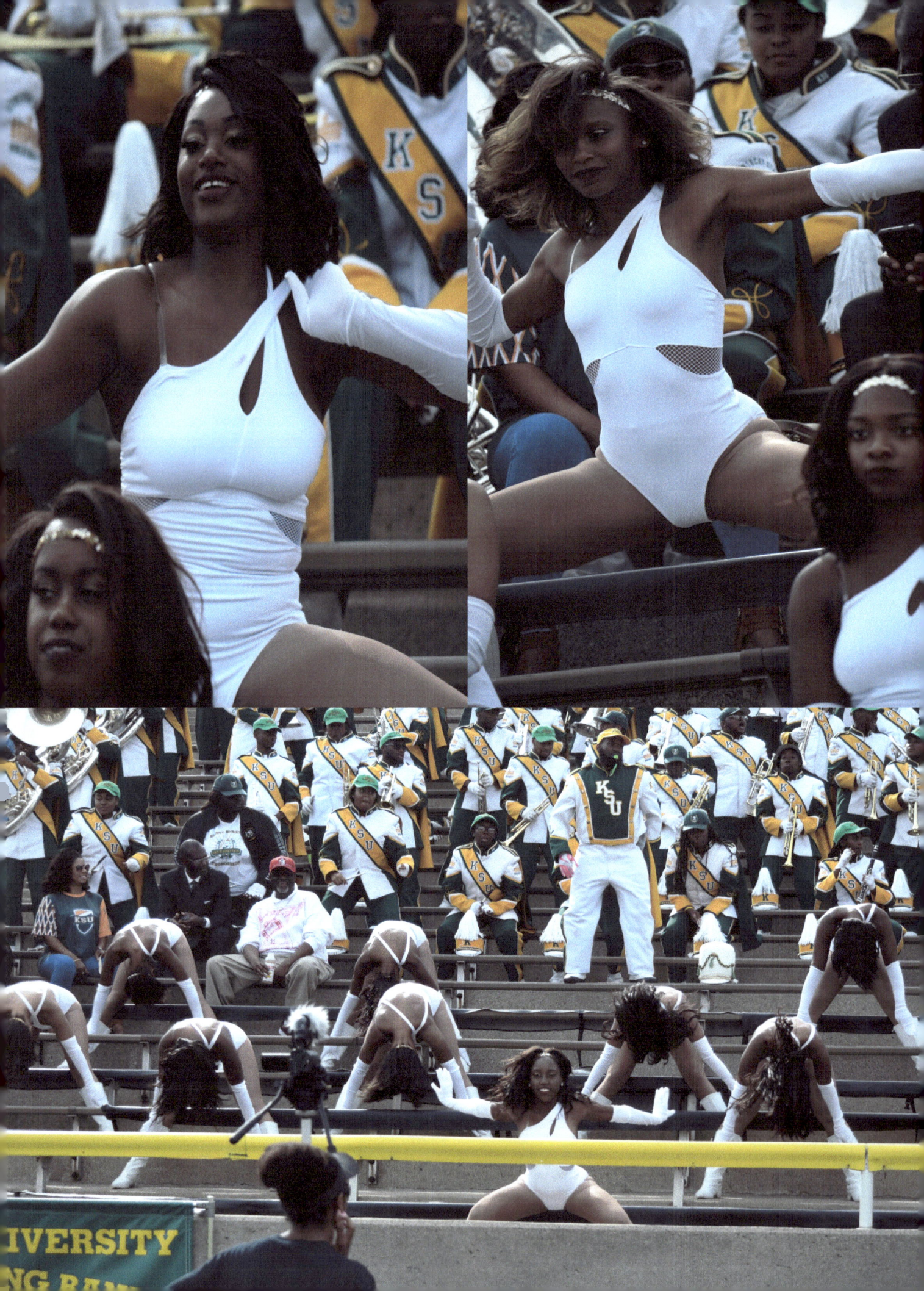

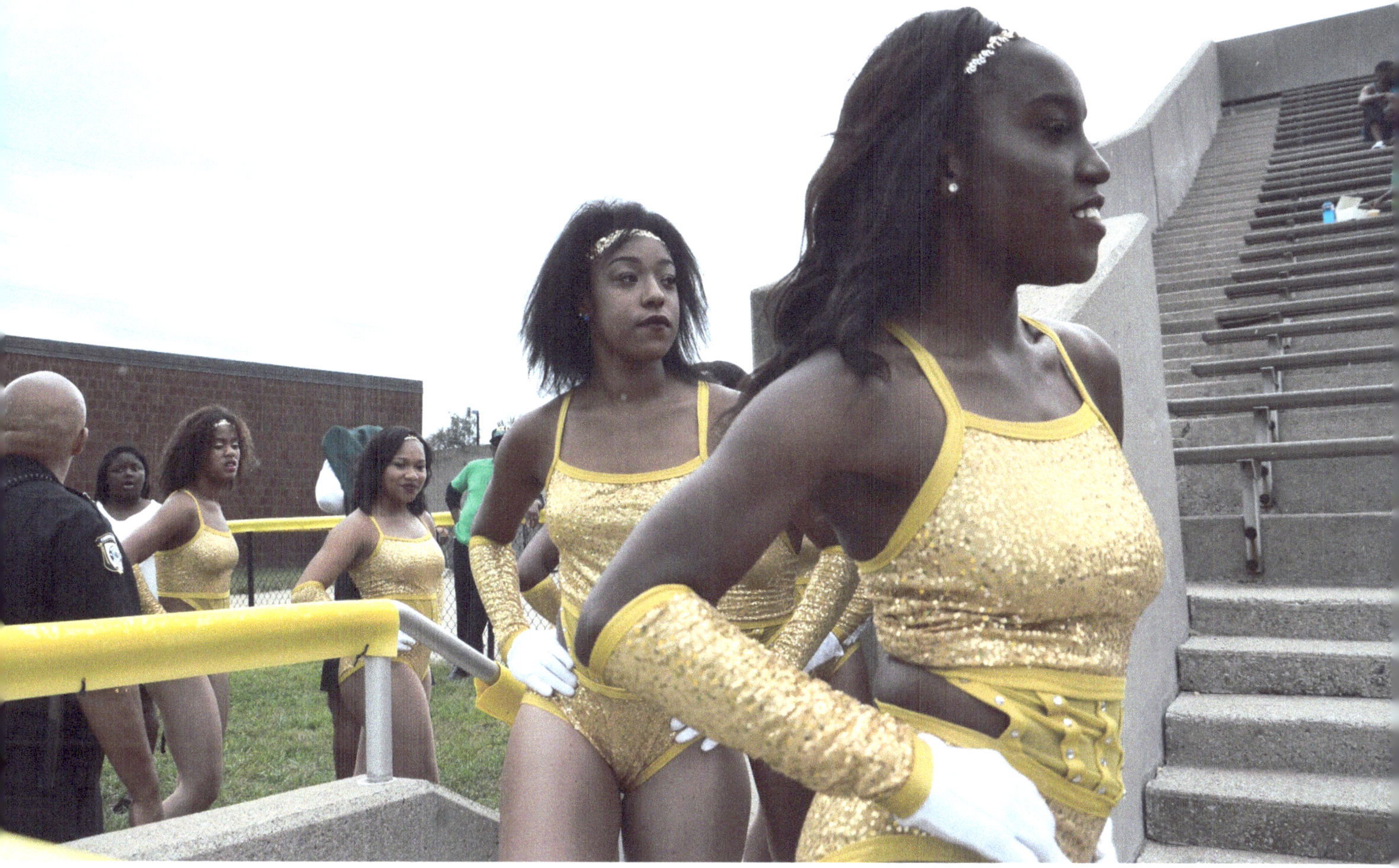

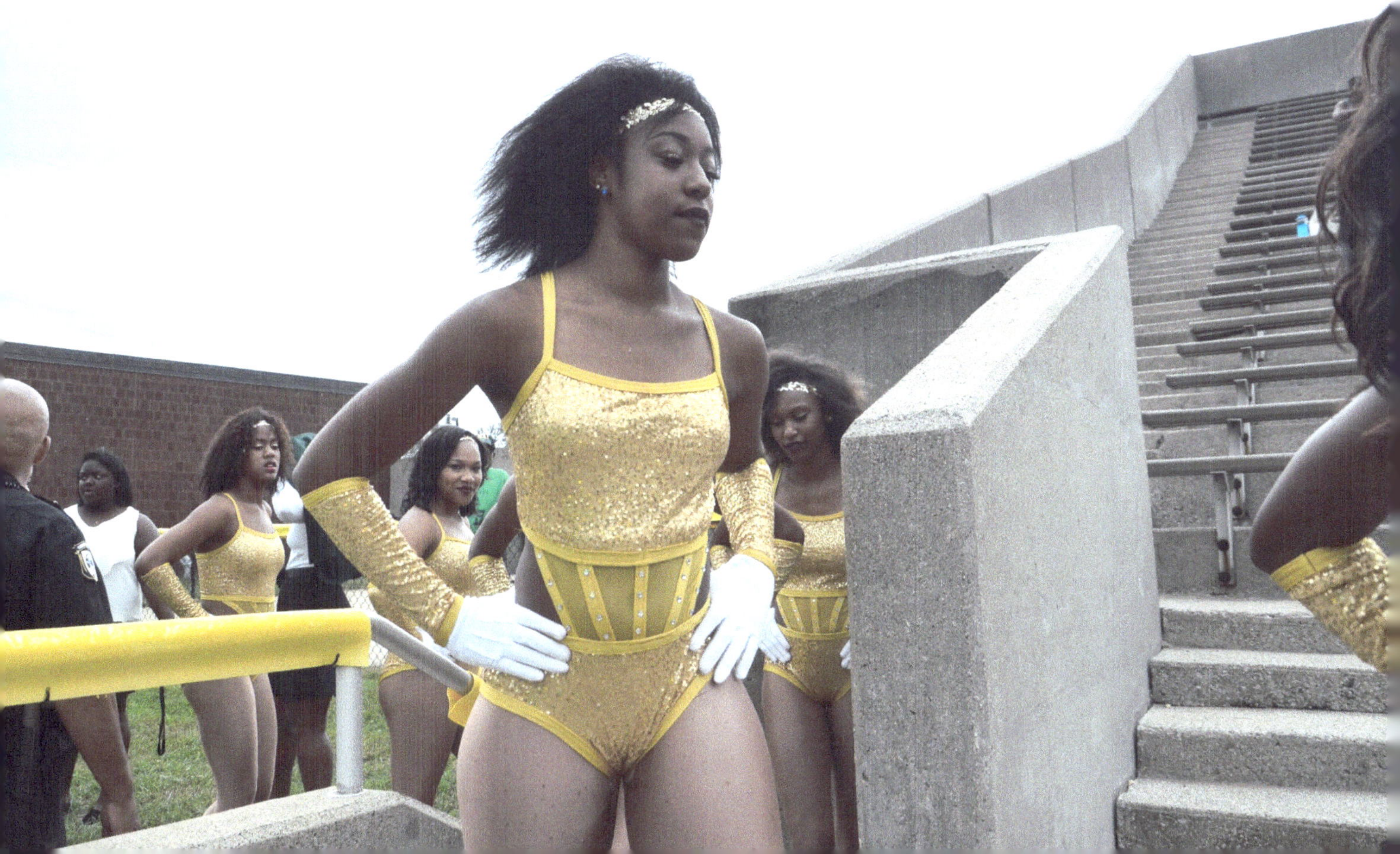

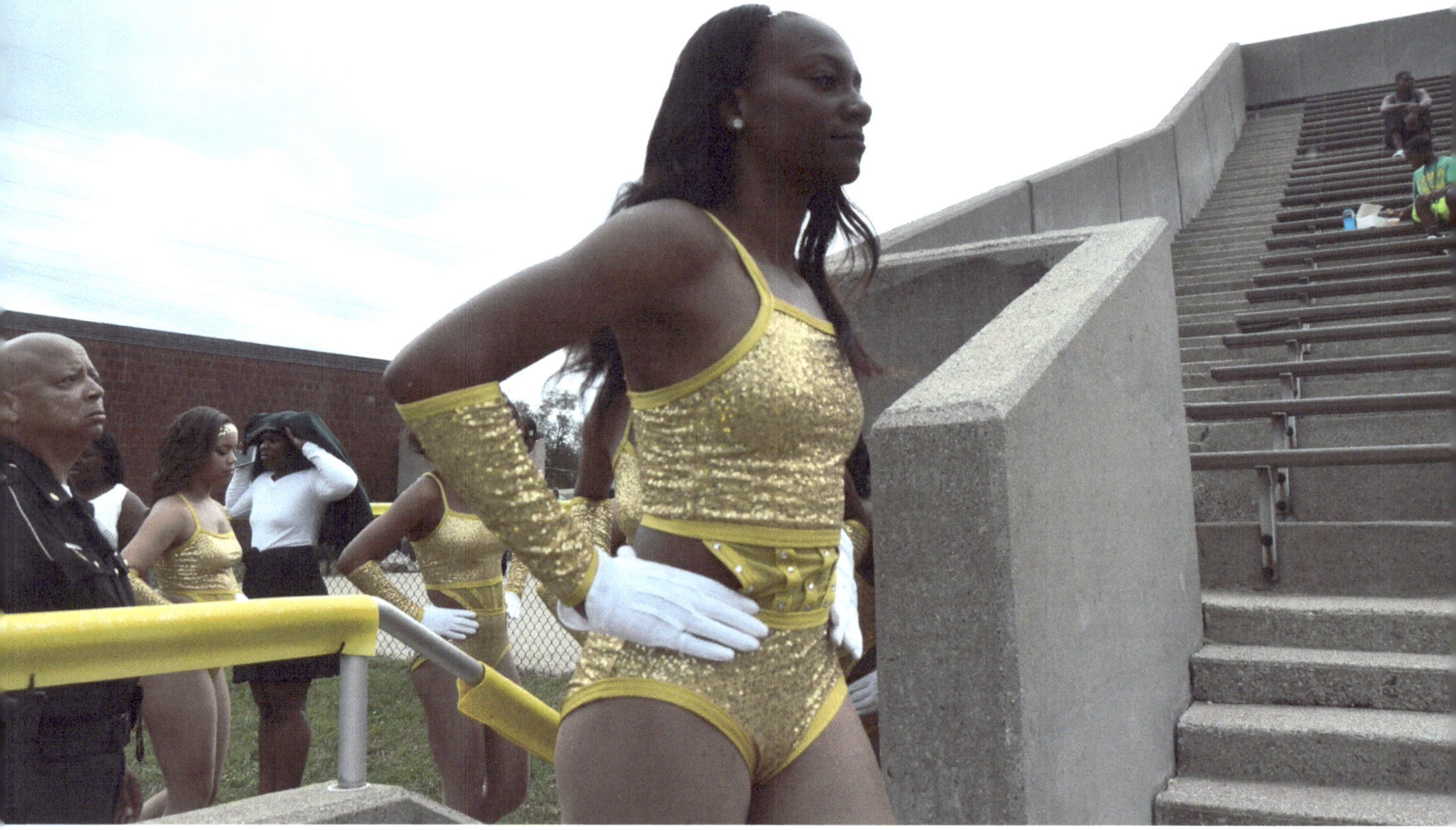

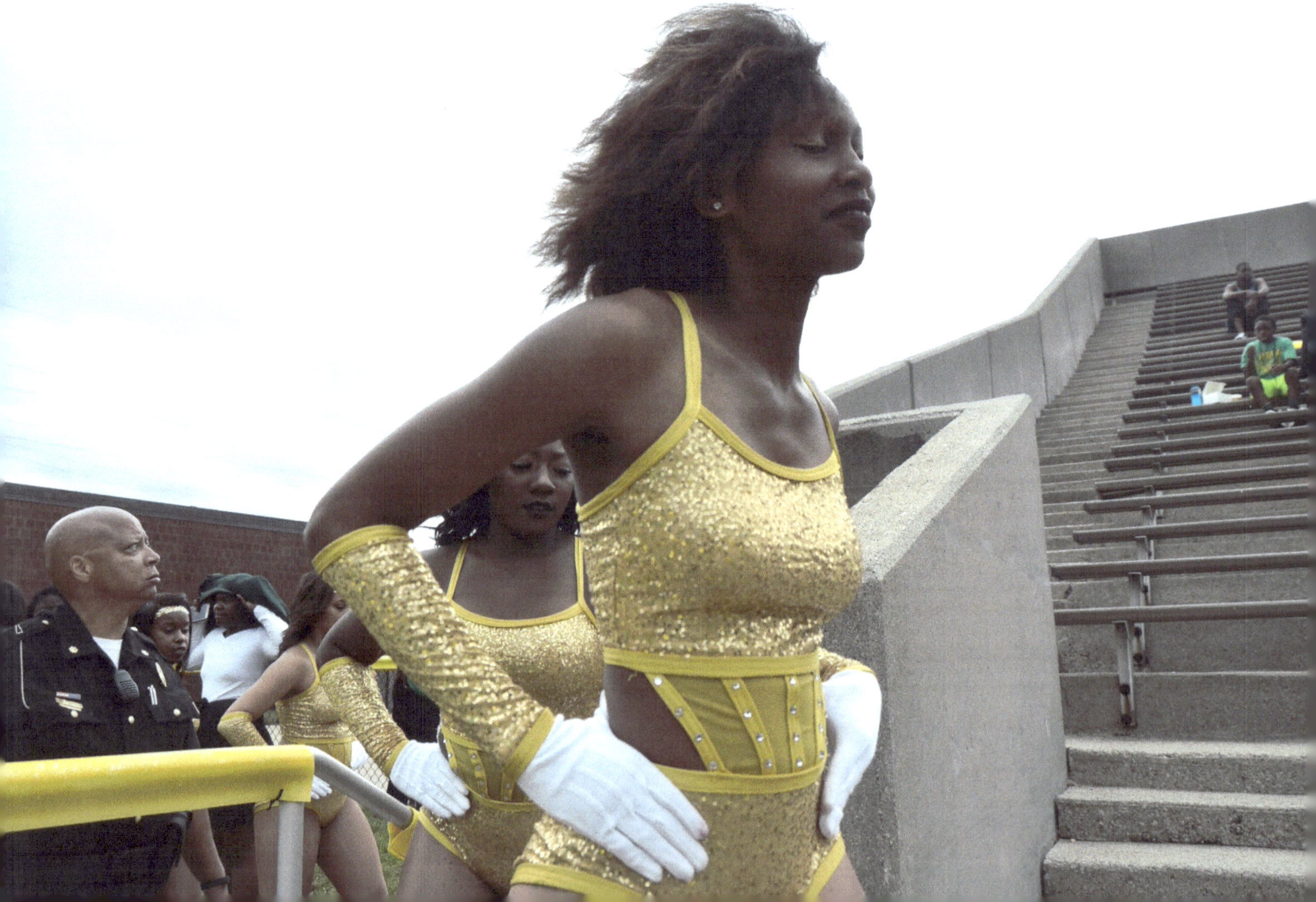

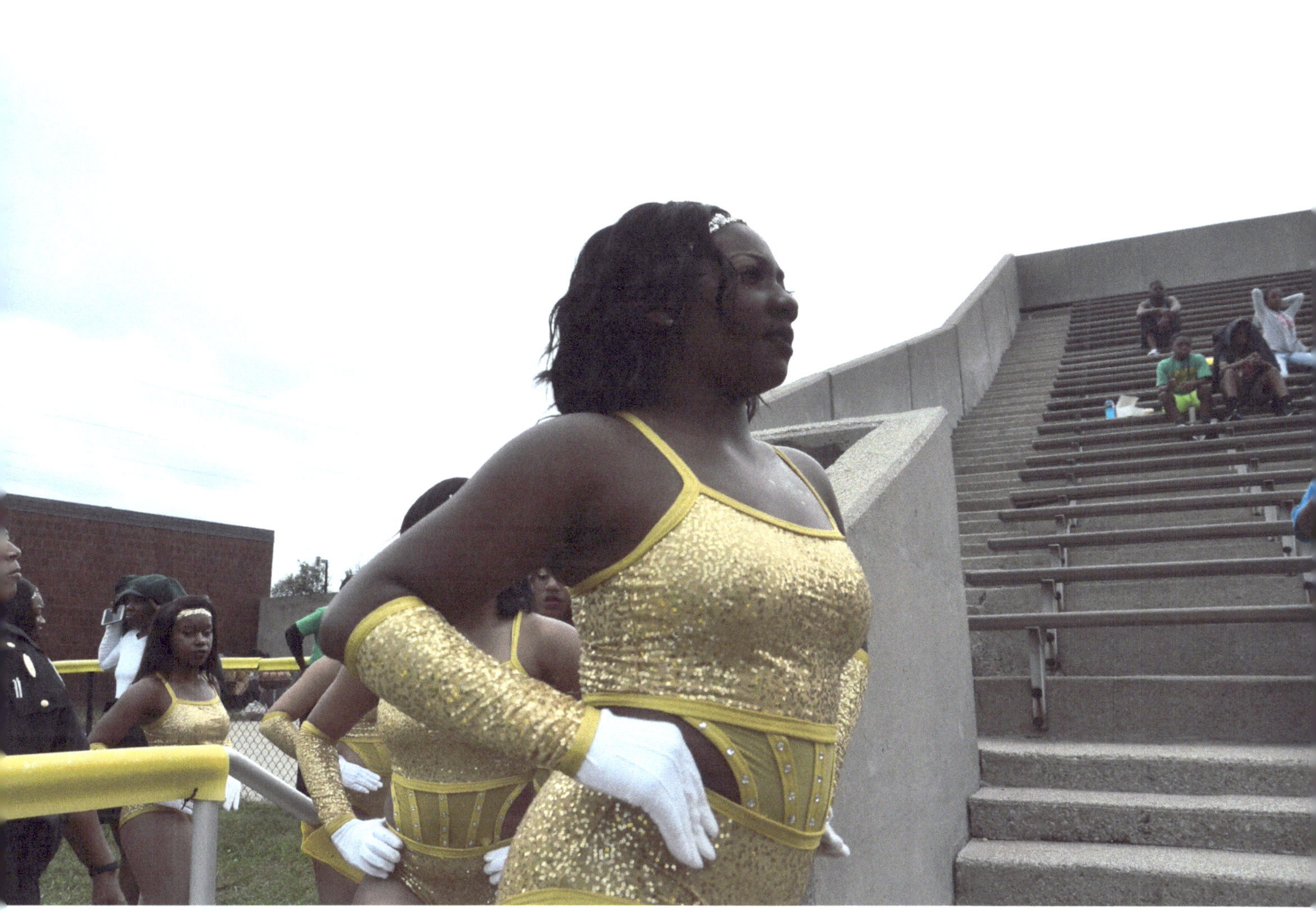

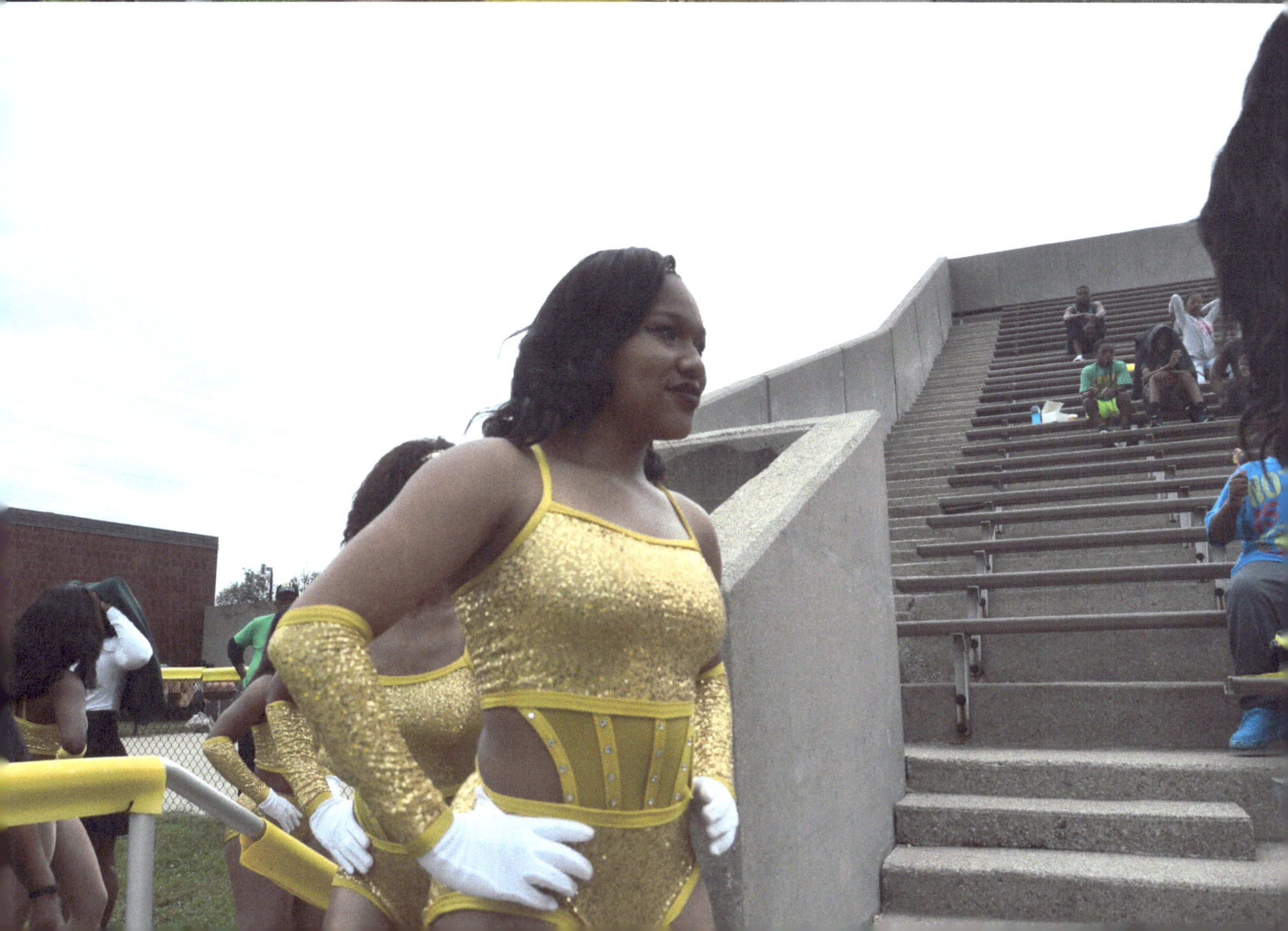

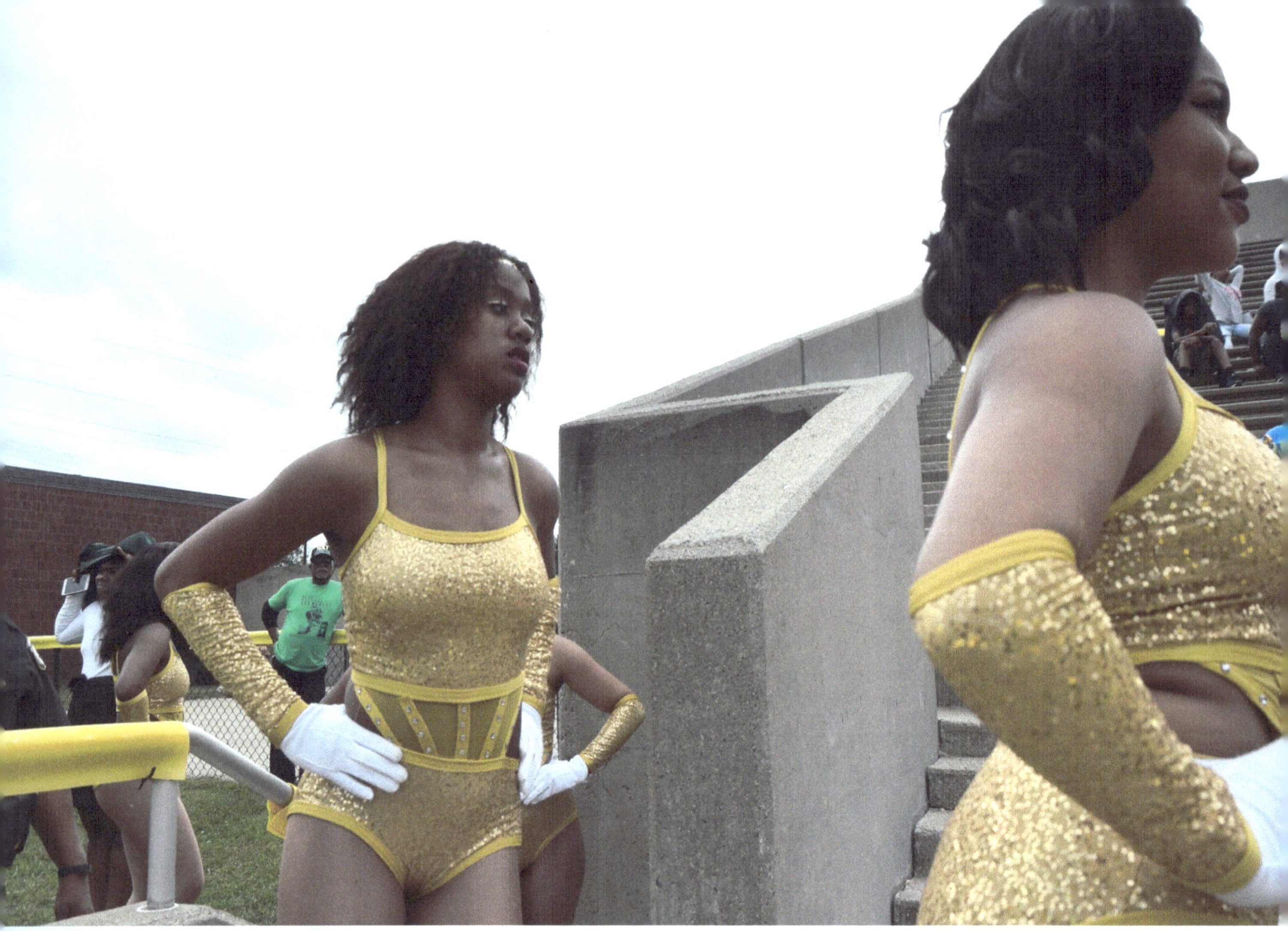

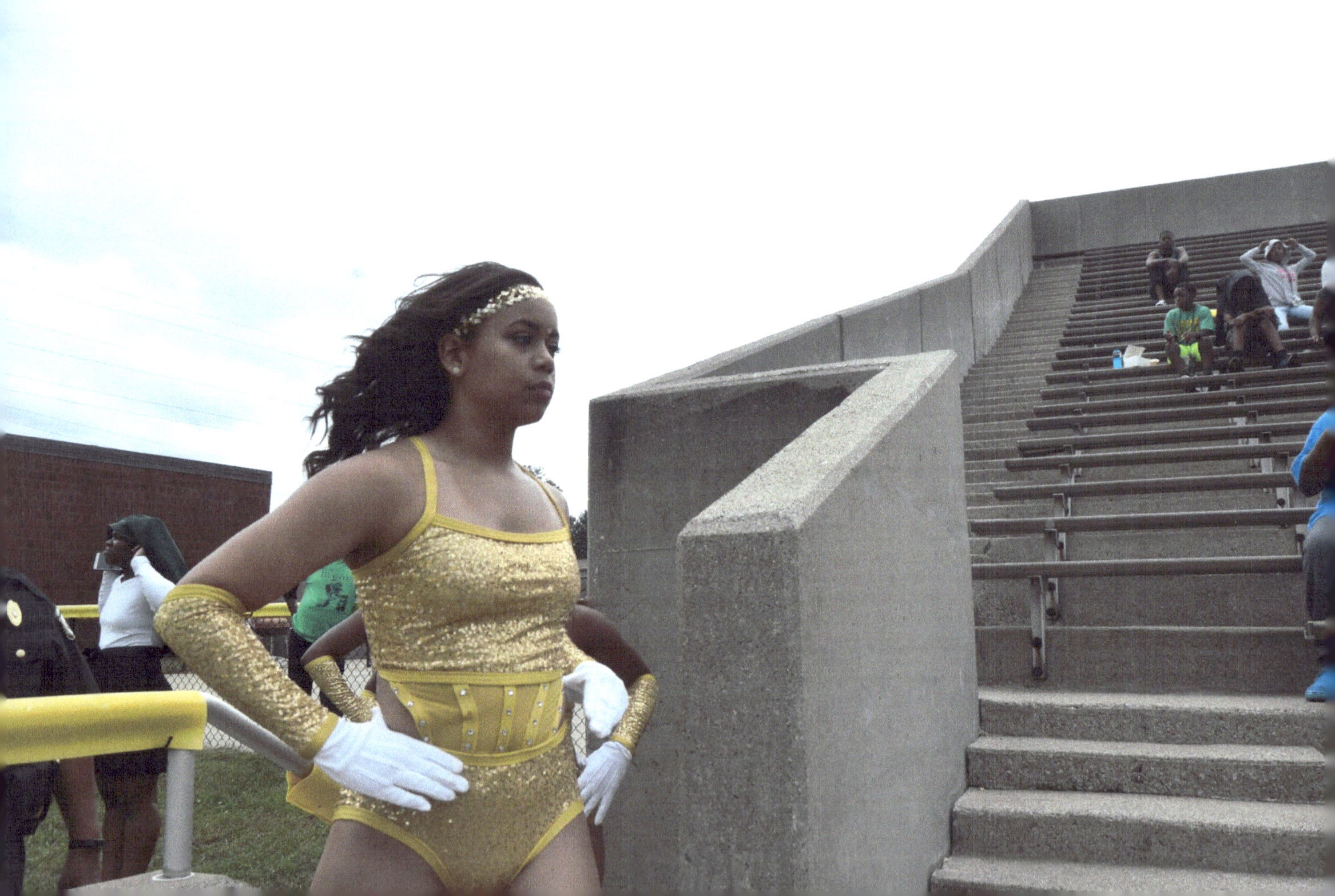

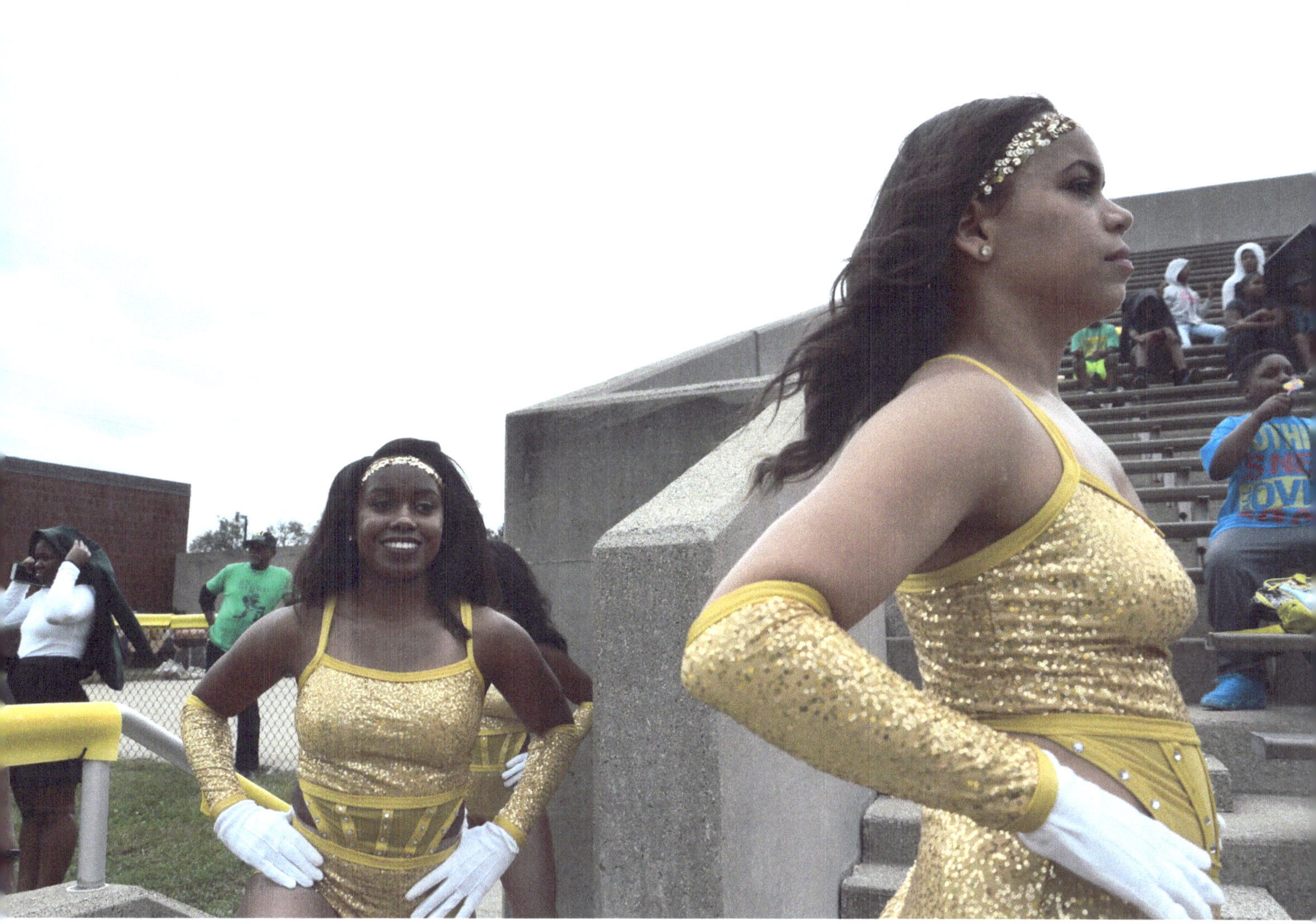

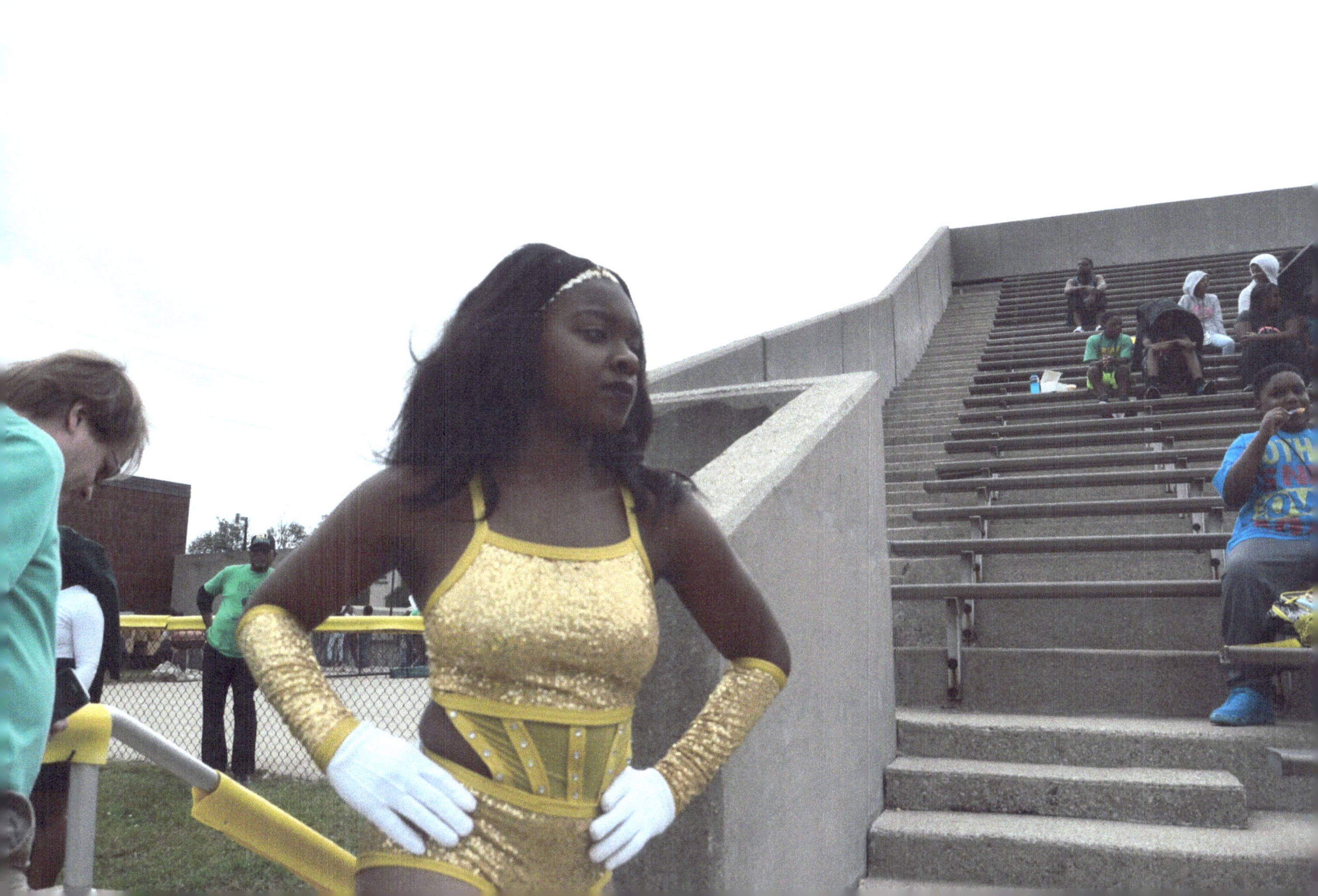

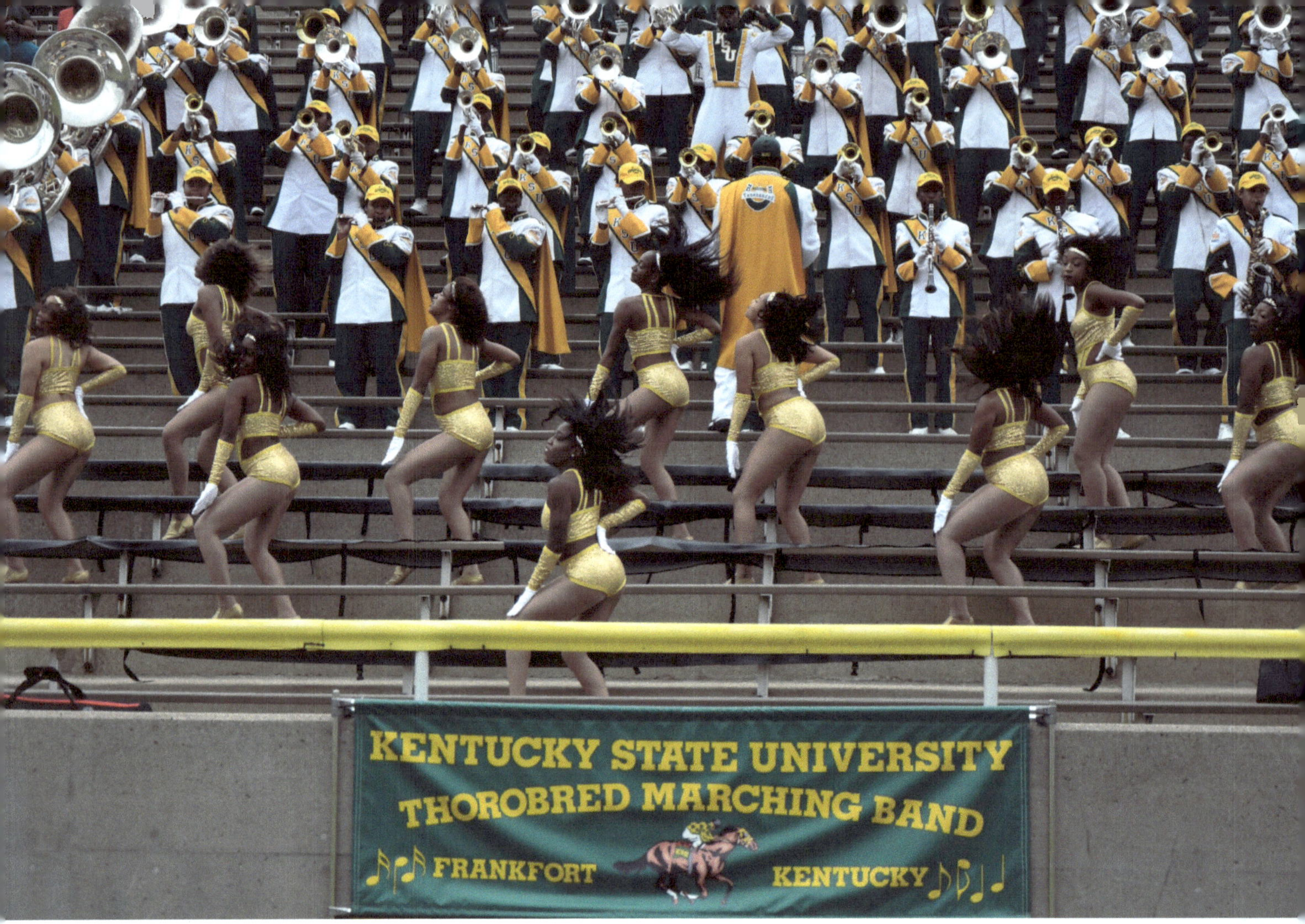

KENTUCKY STATE UNIVERSITY
THOROBRED MARCHING BAND
♪♫♪ FRANKFORT   KENTUCKY ♪♪♩♩

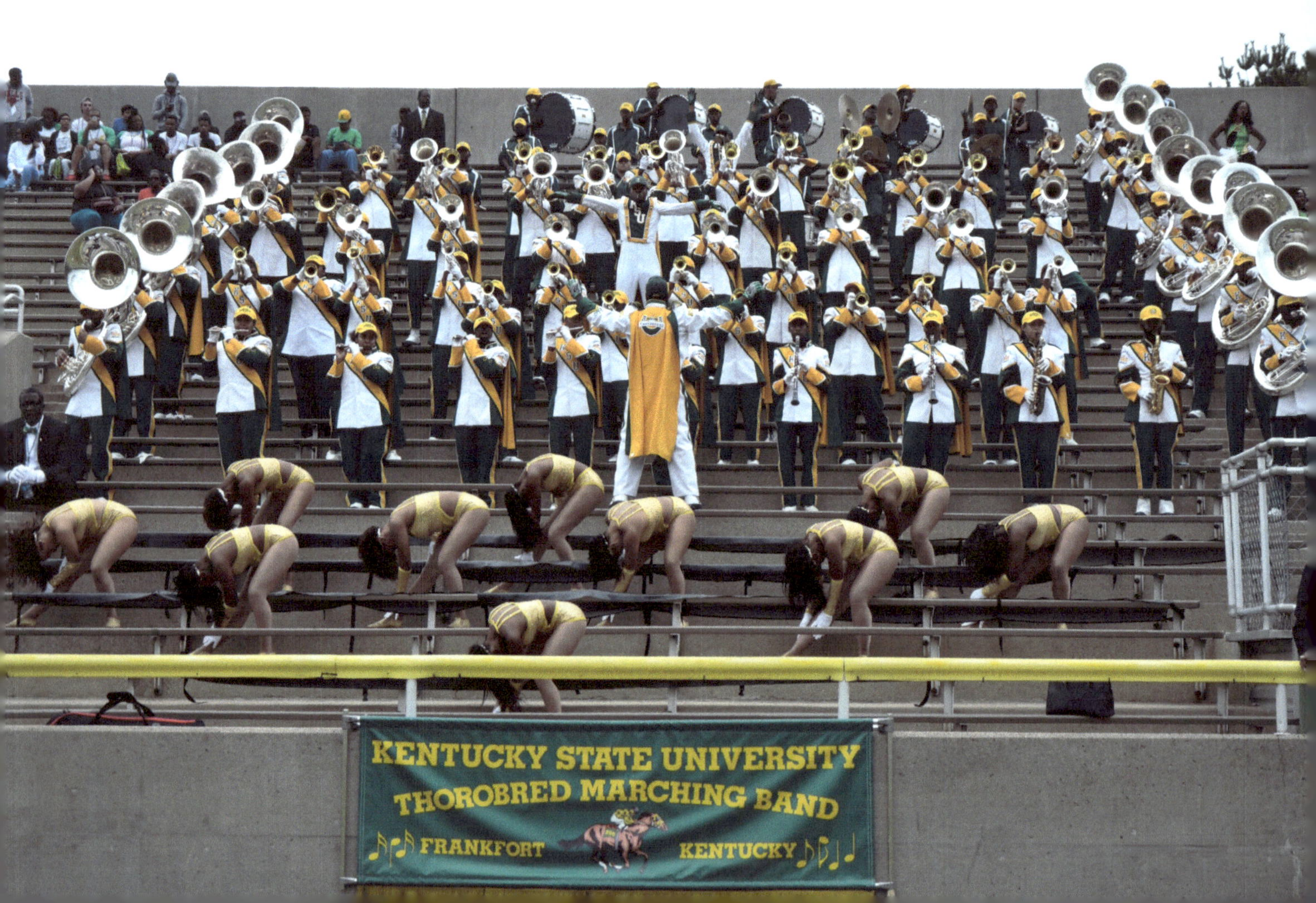

KENTUCKY STATE UNIVERSITY
THOROBRED MARCHING BAND
♪♫♪ FRANKFORT   KENTUCKY ♪♪♩♩

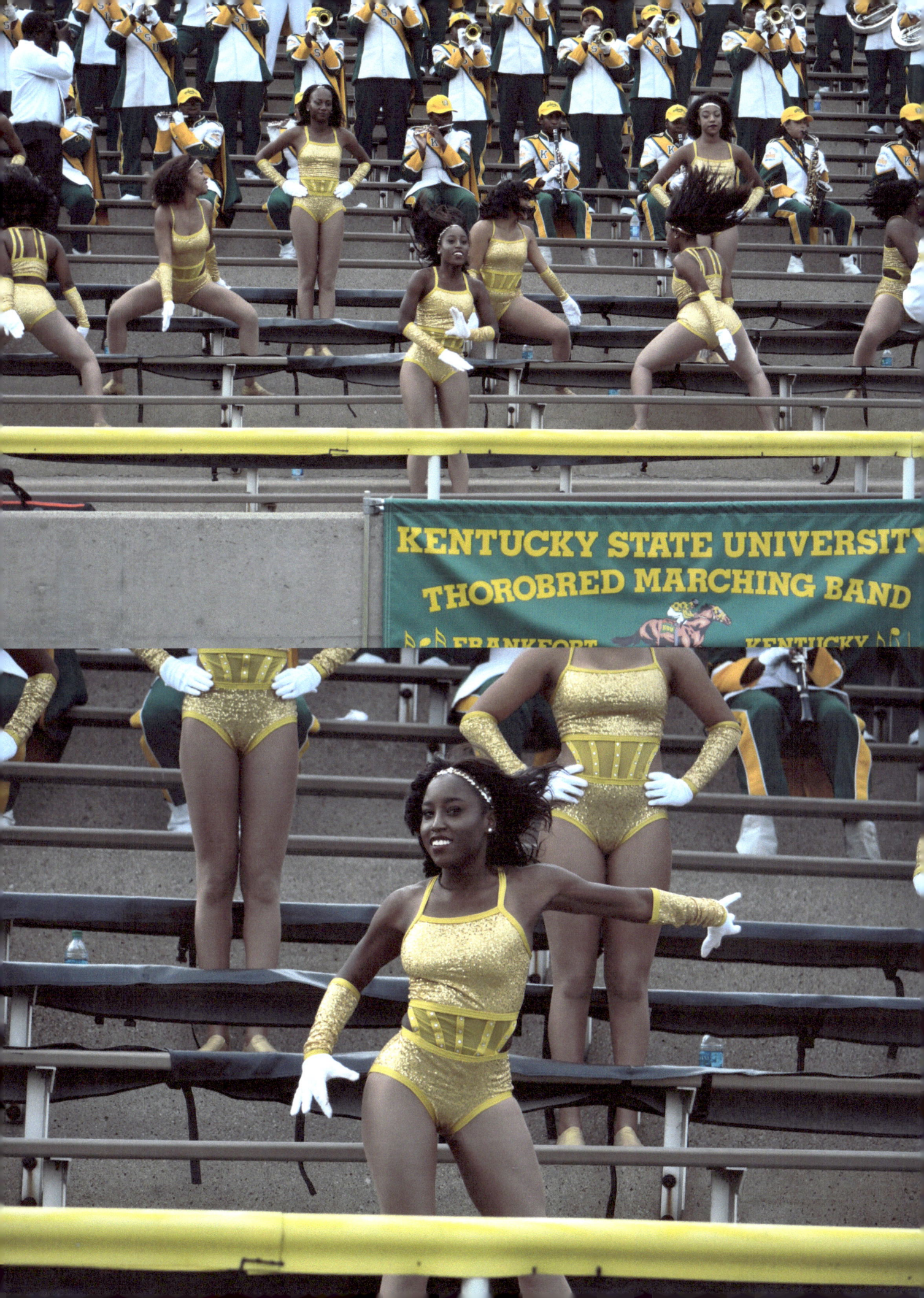

KENTUCKY STATE UNIVERSITY
THOROBRED MARCHING BAND
FRANKFORT · KENTUCKY

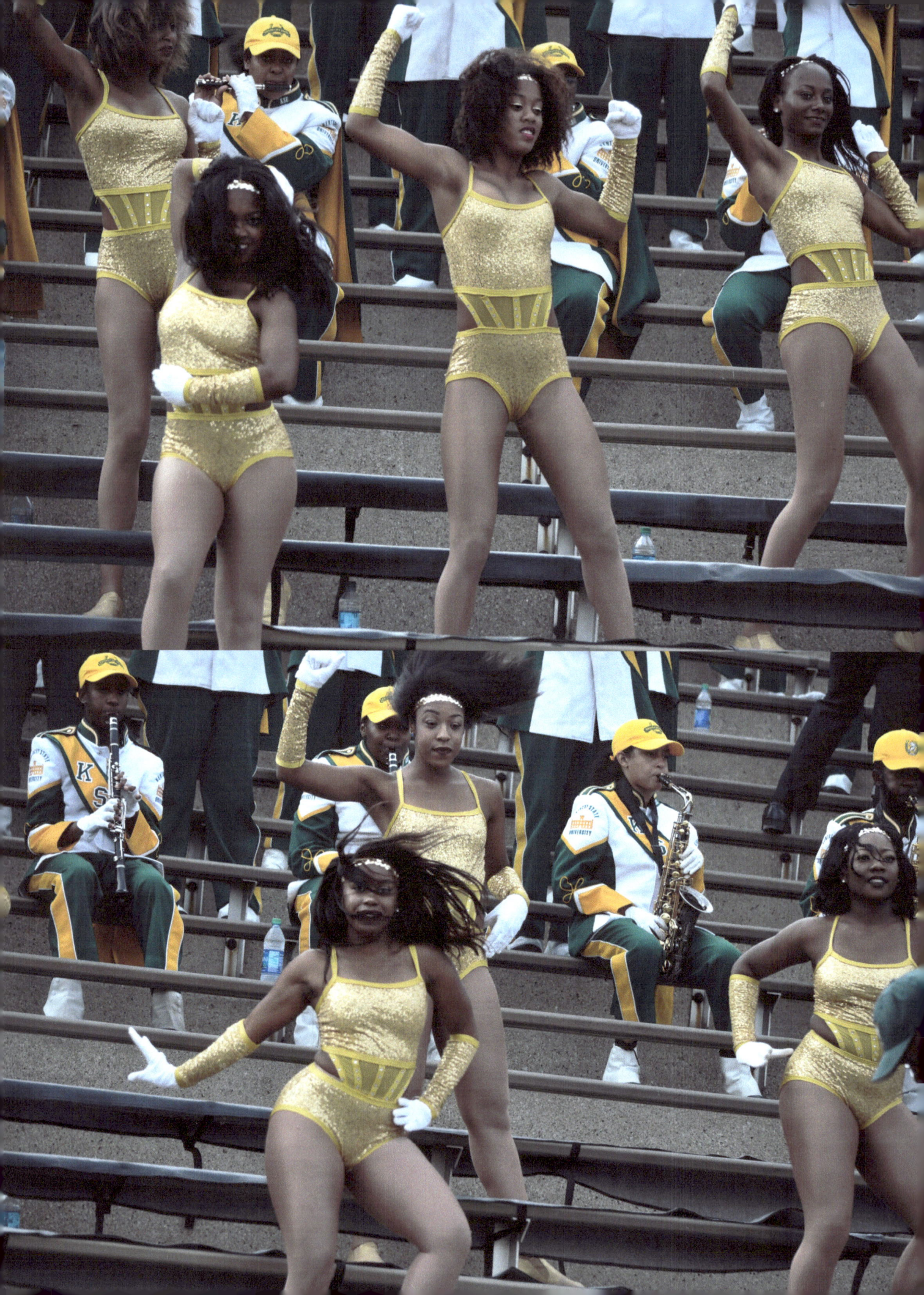

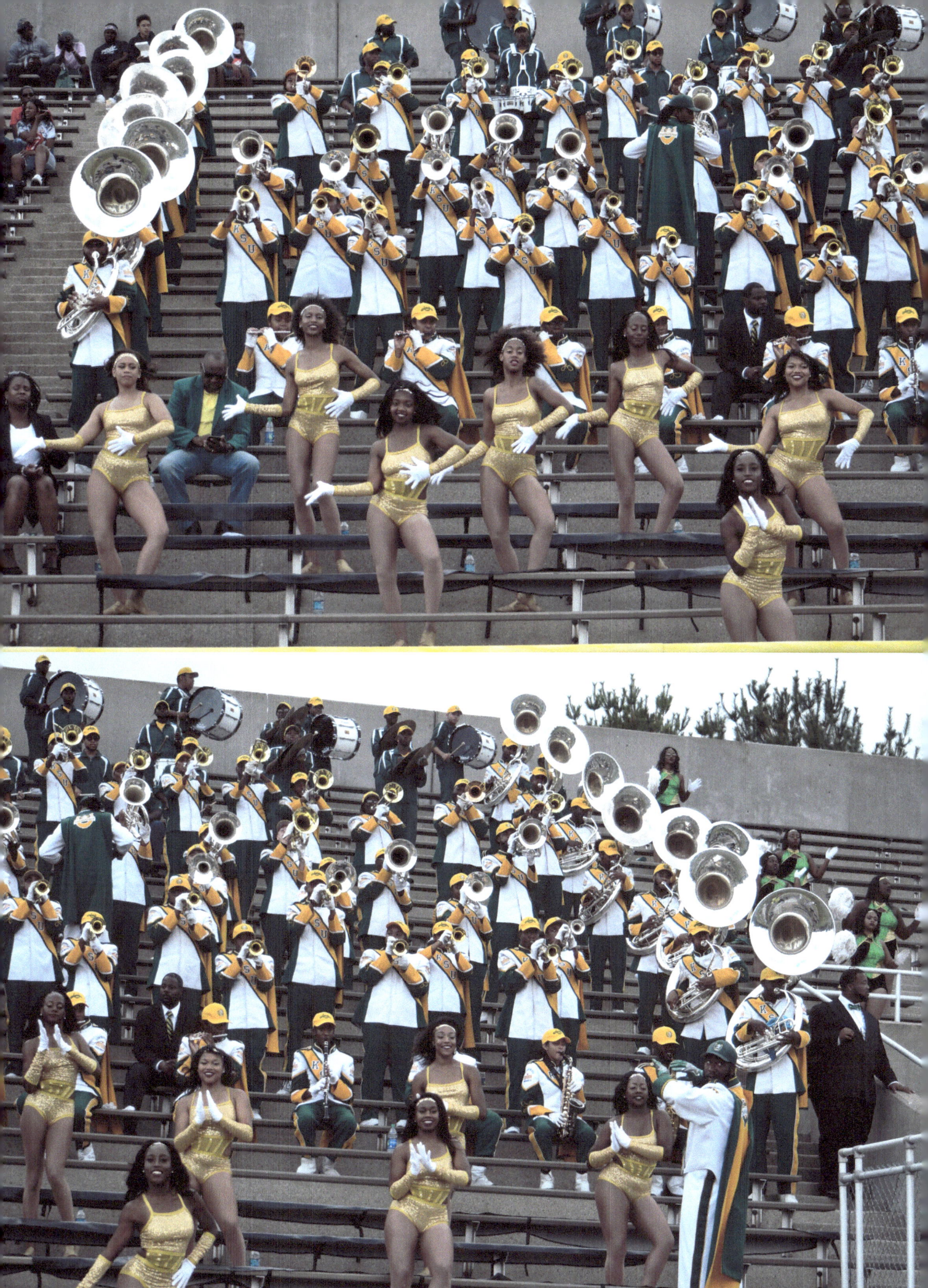

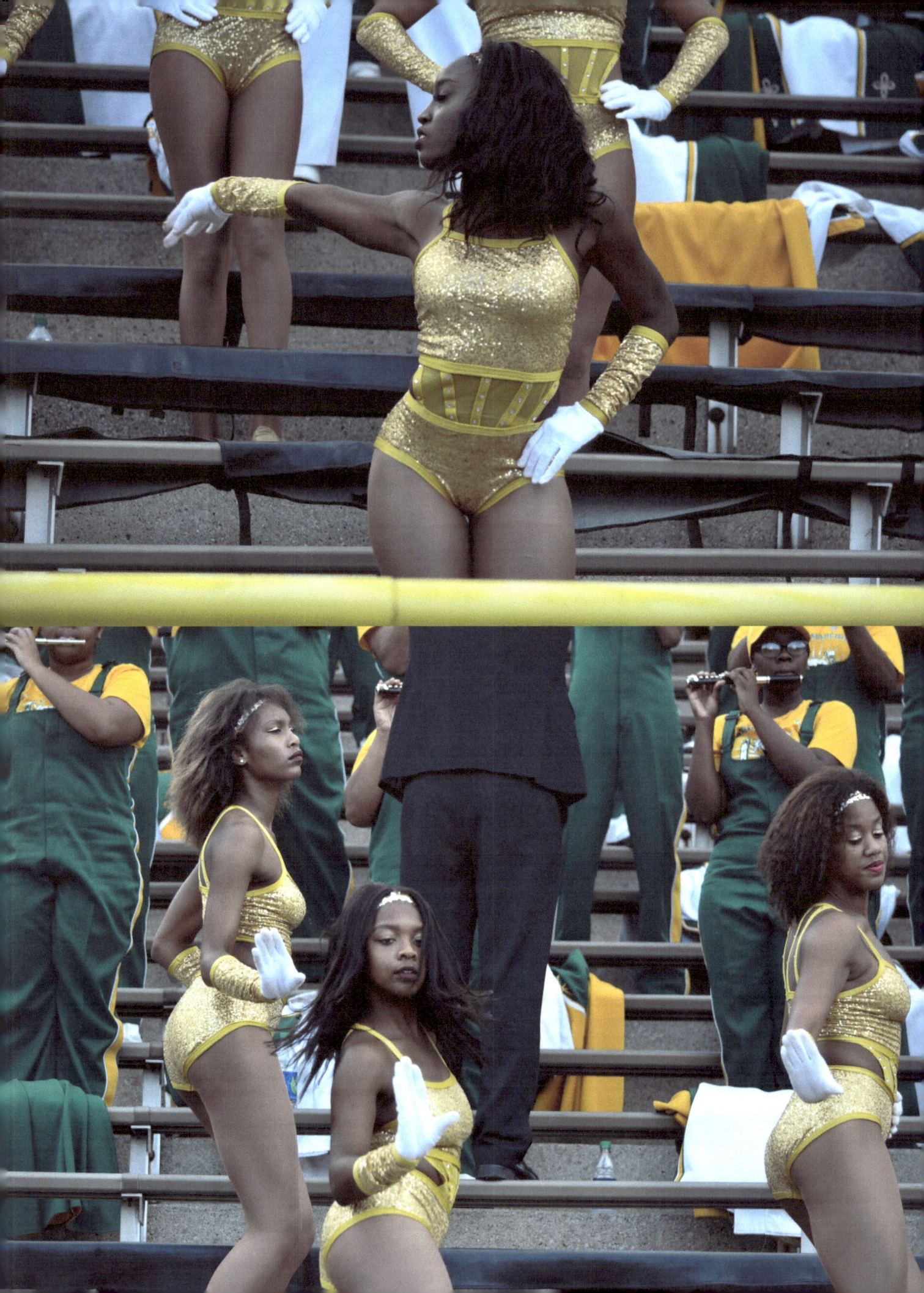

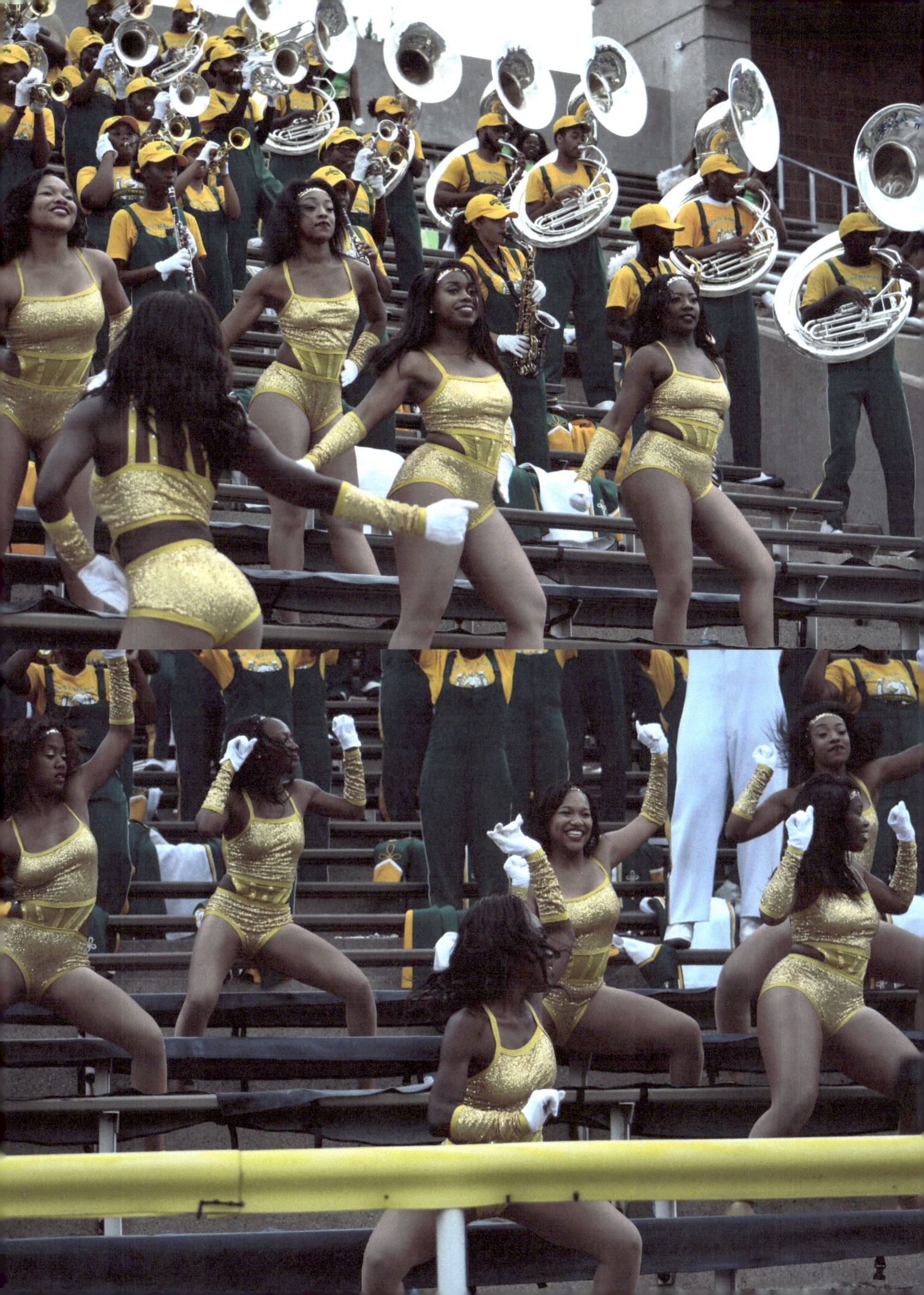

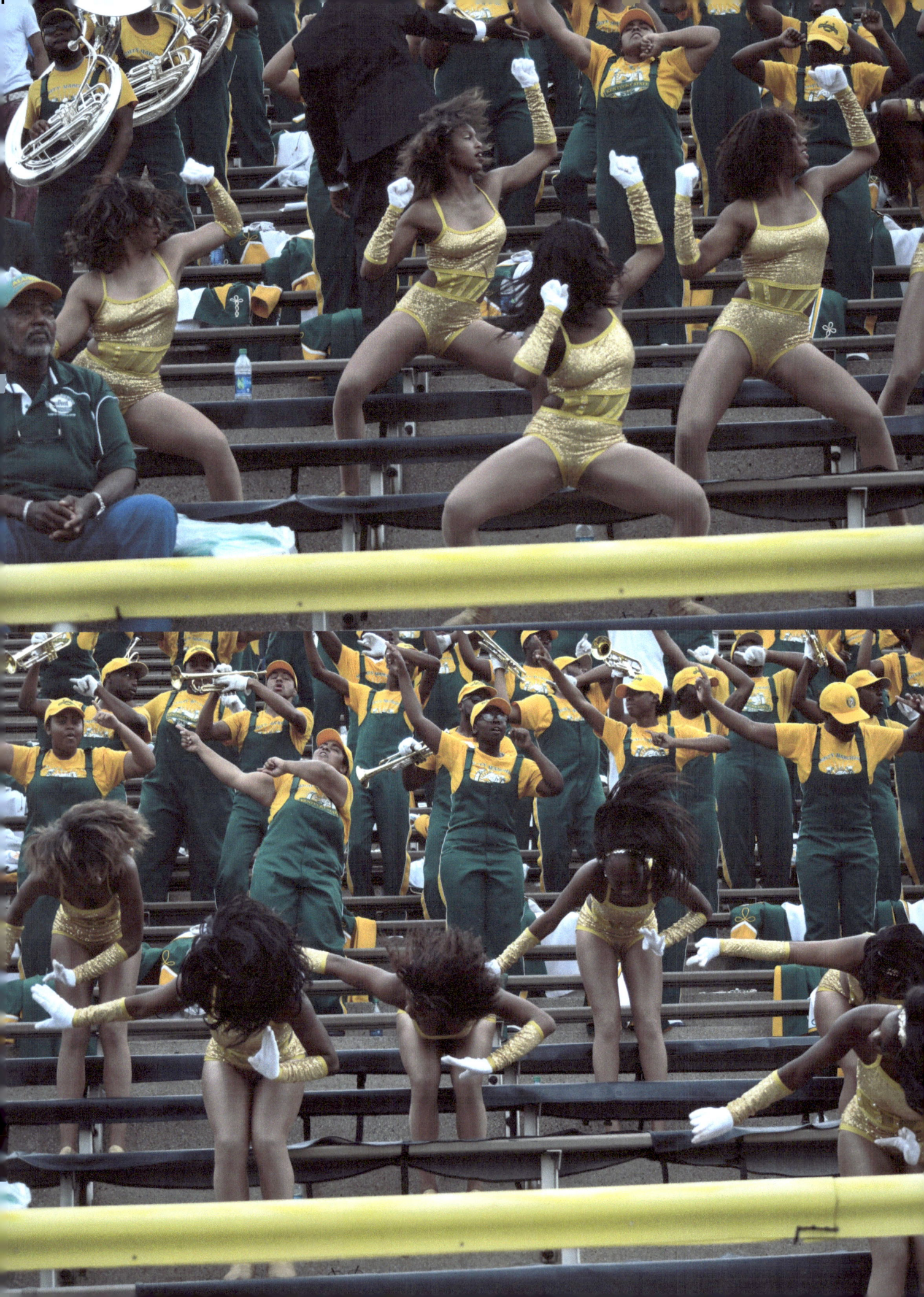

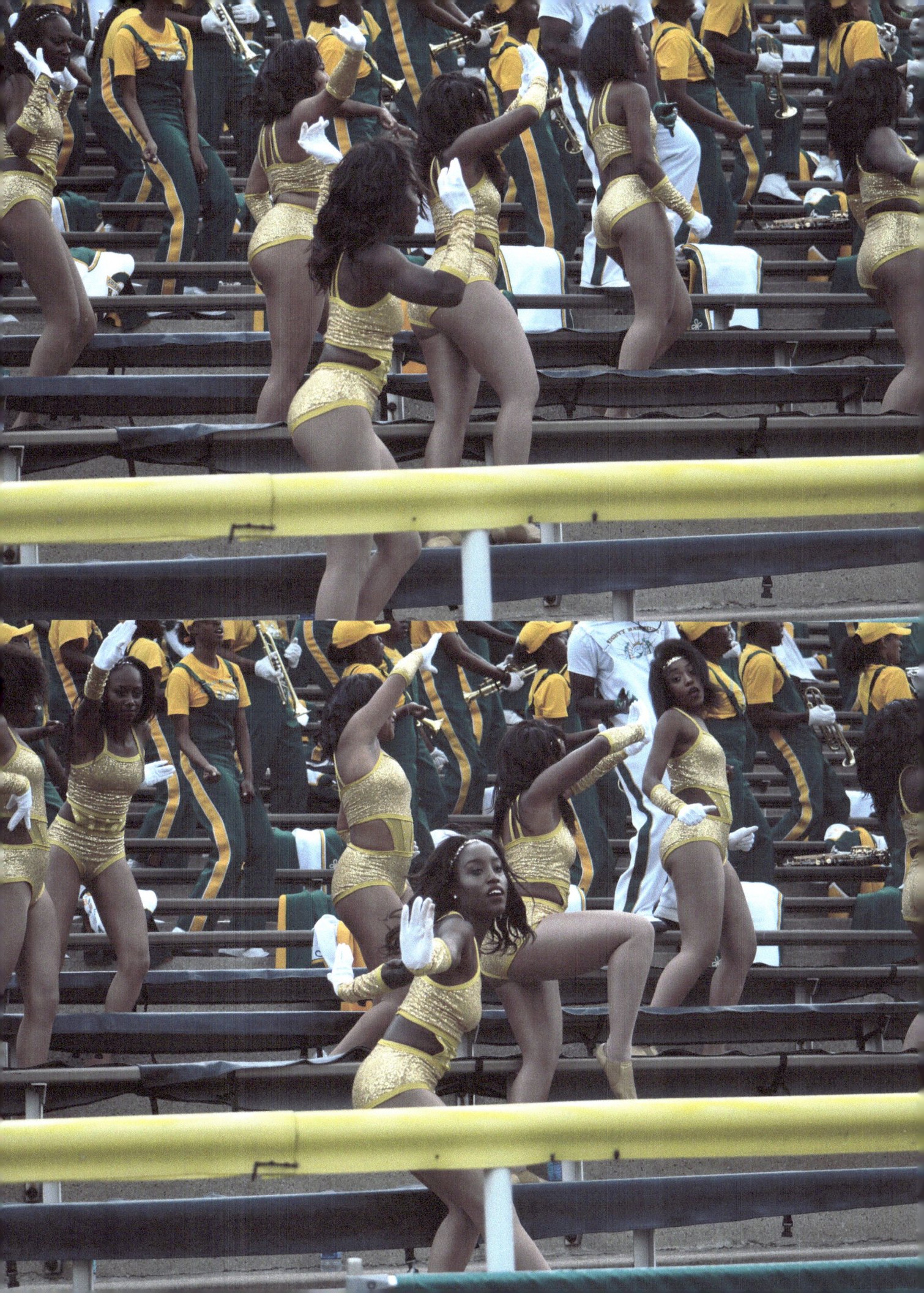

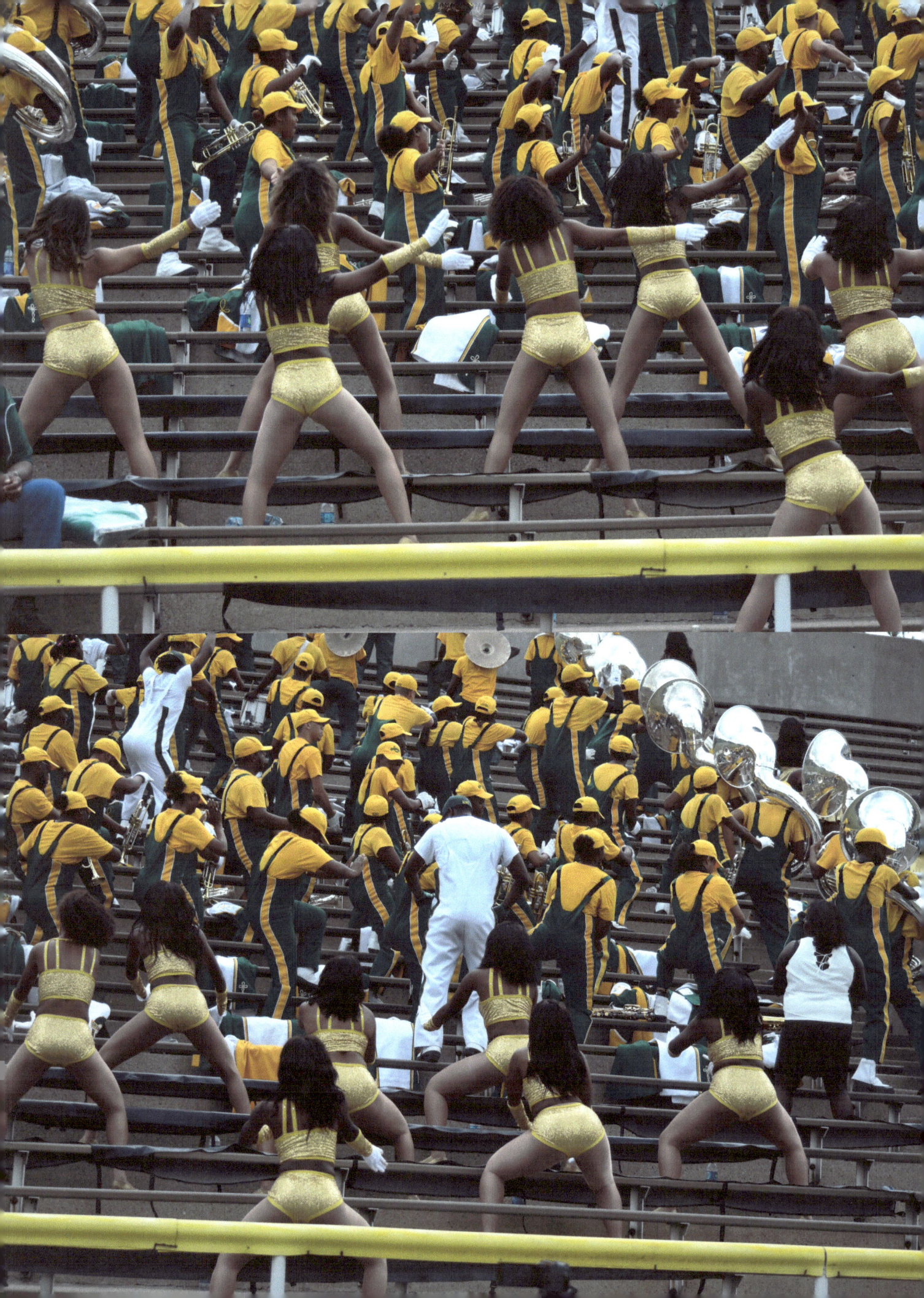

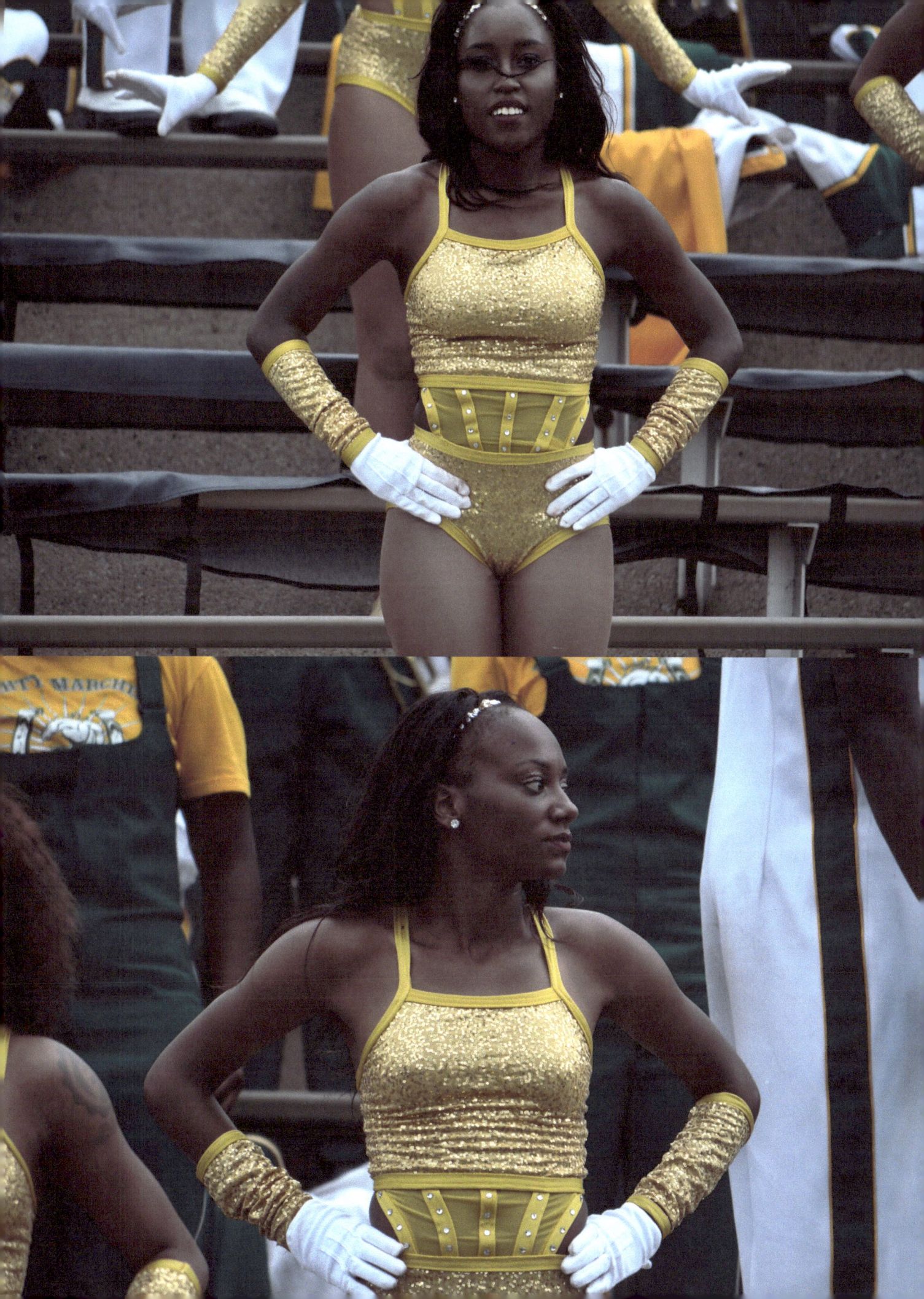

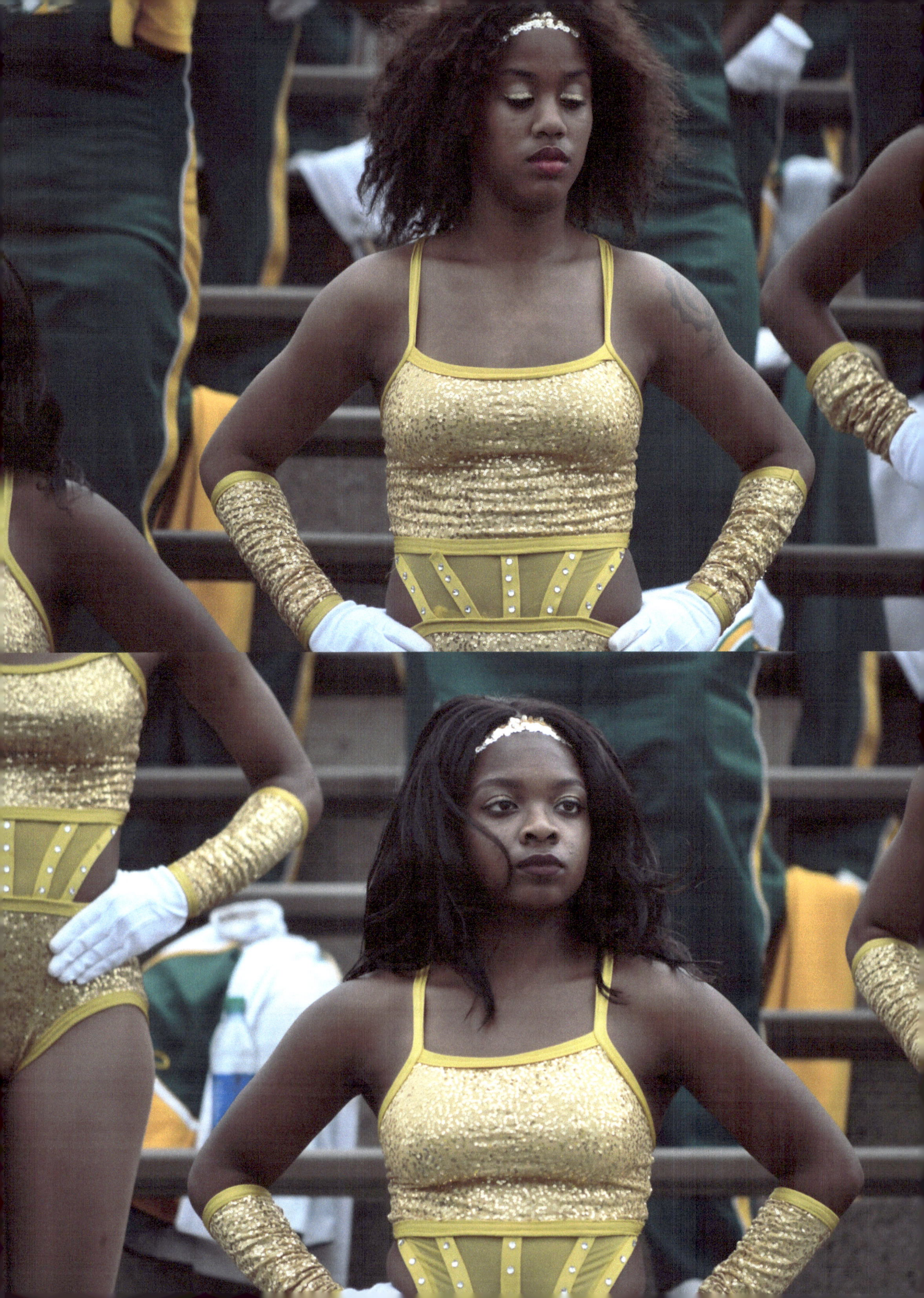

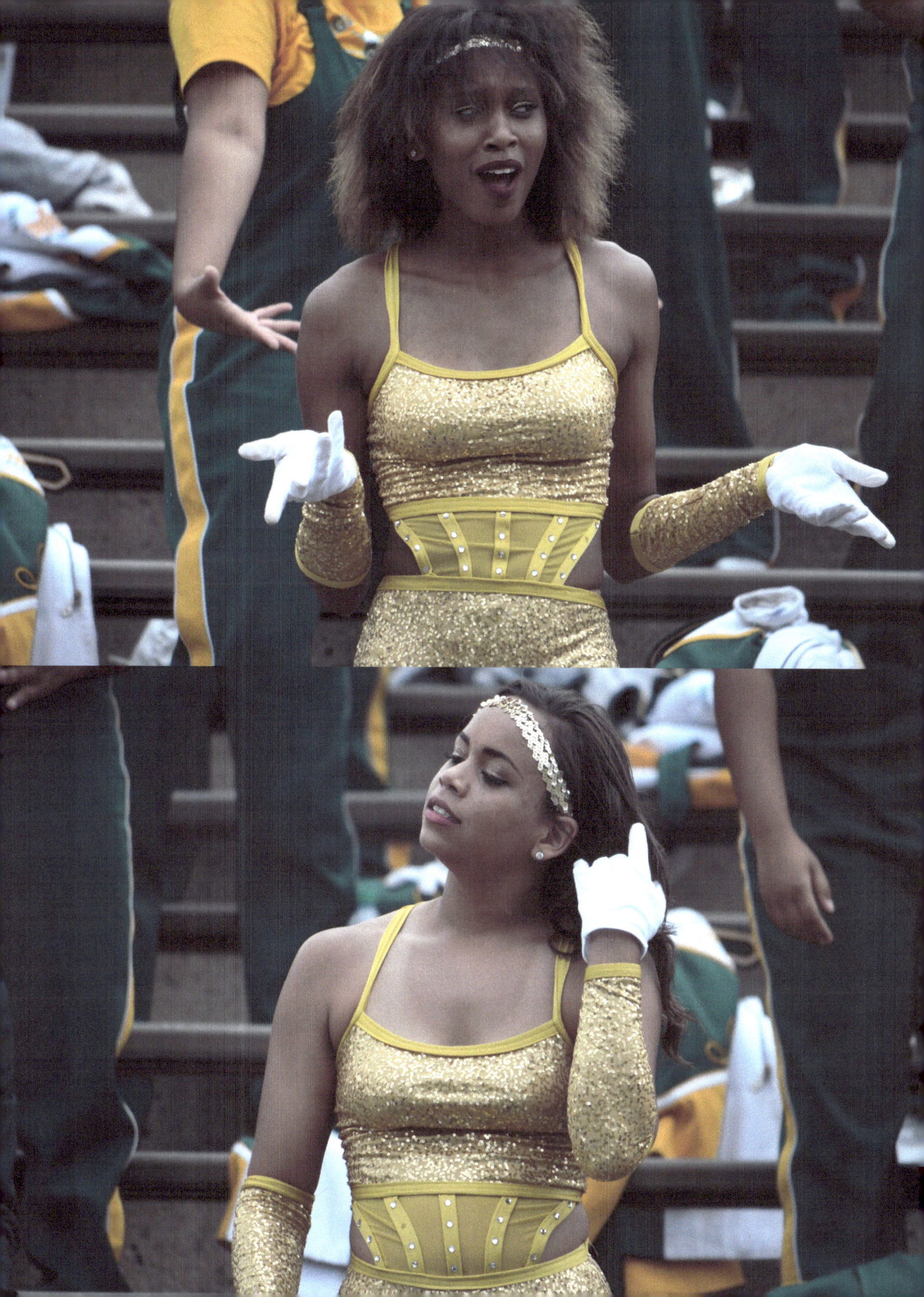

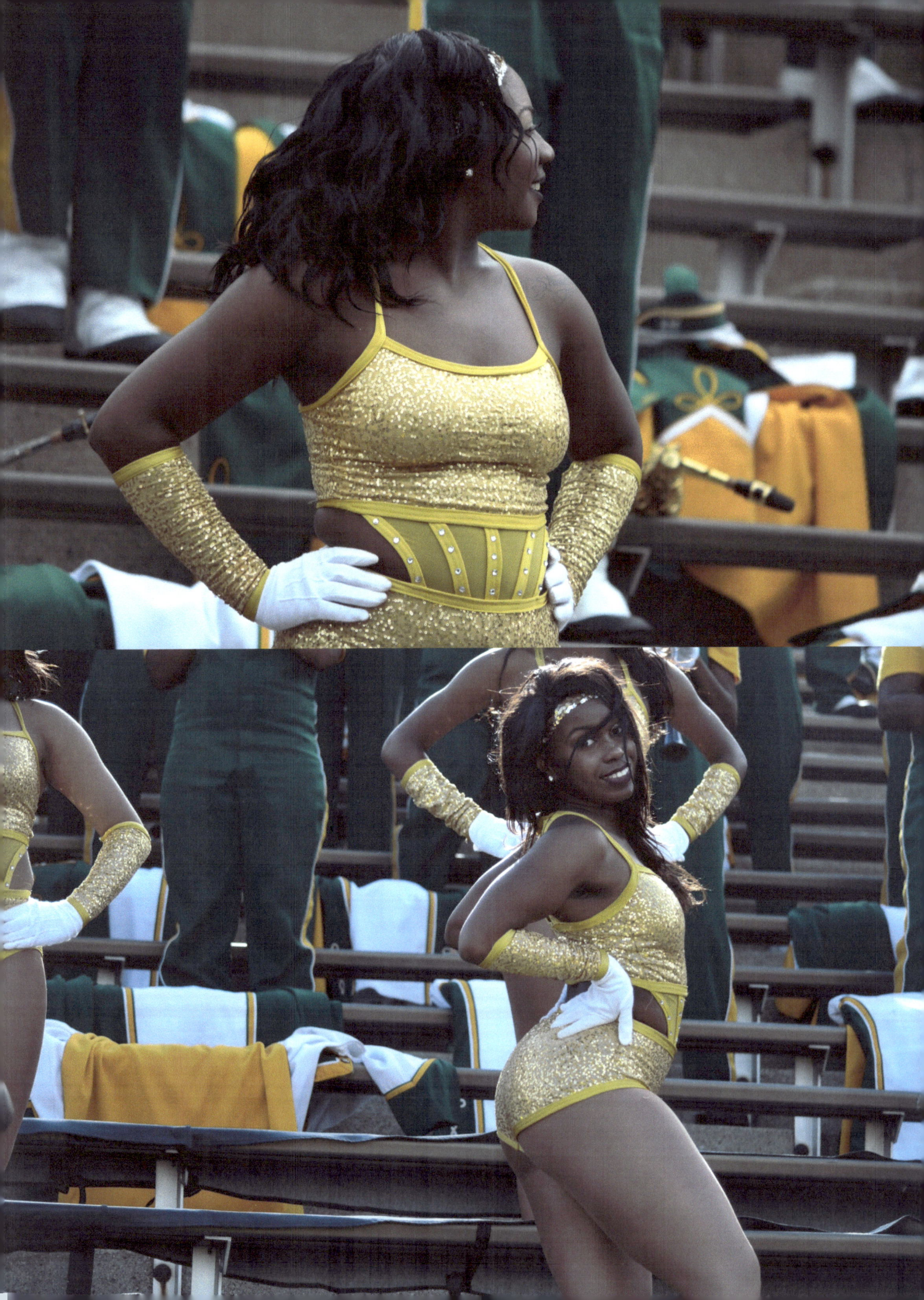

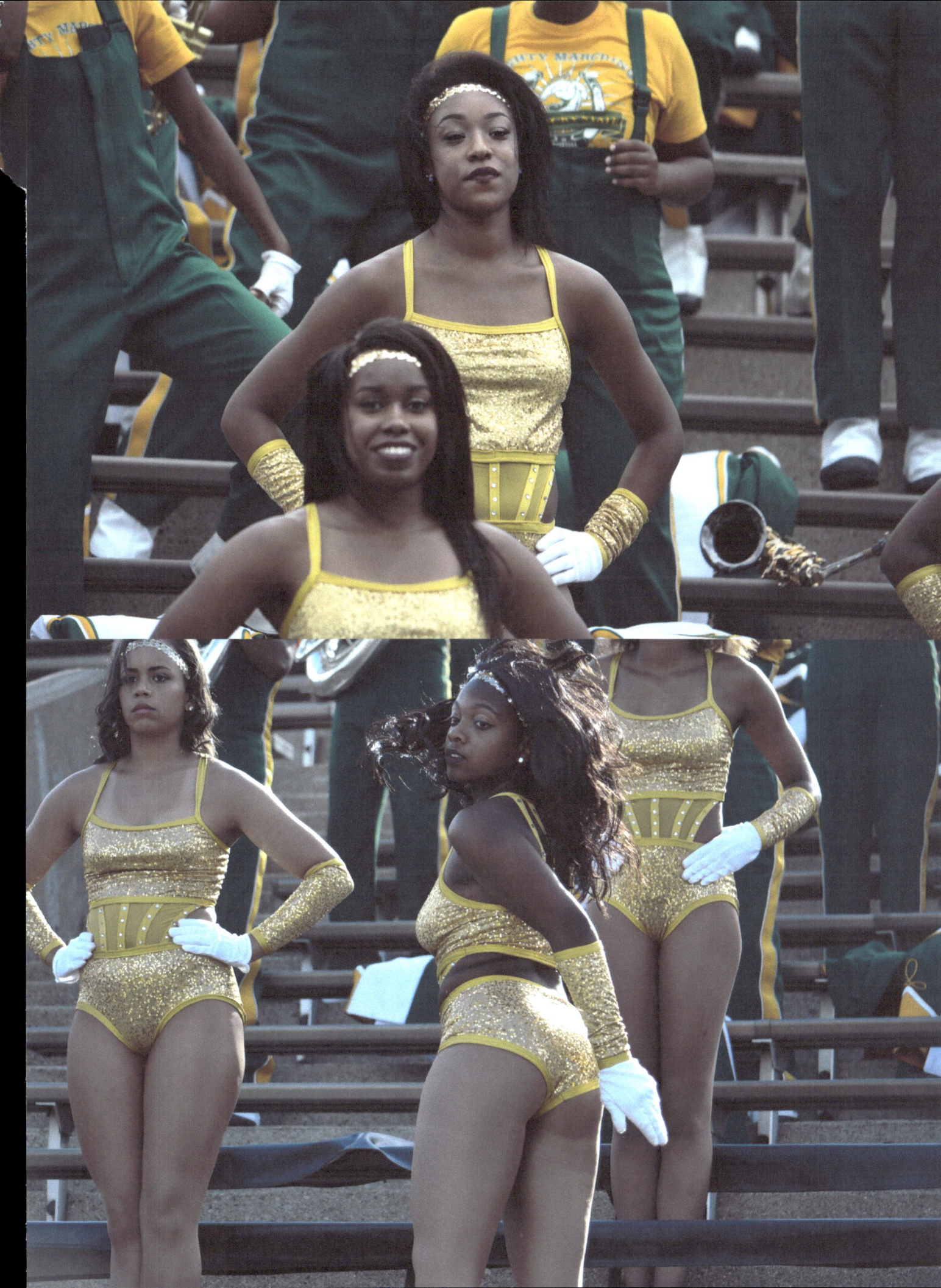

CREDITS AND ACKNOWLEDGEMENTS

ALL PHOTOS BY LACY L. RICE JR. OF NBEI PHOTOGRAPHY

ACKNOWLEDGEMENTS AT KENTUCKY STATE UNIVERSITY DURING FALL 2017;
DR. M. CHRISTOPHER BROWN, PRESIDENT
MR. AL LEVEL, DIRECTOR OF BANDS
MRS. CHURI LEVEL, DIRECTOR OF BAND AUXILIARY
DR. ROOSEVELT SHELTON, CHAIR, MUSIC DEPARTMENT
MR. WILLIAM GRAHAM, ATHLETIC DIRECTOR
MR. ERIC MATTHEWS, SPORTS INFORMATION DIRECTOR
THE MIGHTY MARCHING THOROBREDS AND K-RETTES

THANKS TO ALL OF OUR FANS AND SUPPORTERS OVER THE YEARS. THIS PUBLICATION MARKS THE
BEGINNING OF THINGS TO COME. IMPROVEMENTS WILL OCCUR. SPECIAL THANKS GO TO:
DR. KAREN BEARDEN
MR. ISADORE RICH, THE ONLY TRUE VOICE OF THE KSU THOROBREDS MARCHING BAND
MR. RON BANKS
MS. STEPHANIE KIRKLEY
MR. STEPHEN "BIG" TATE
MS. CHRISTINA COLEMAN
MR. OSCAR WOODALL OF HAYWOOD MEDIA
MR. BRIAN EVANS, AD AT GEORGETOWN COLLEGE
MR. CURTIS CAMPBELL, AD AT WESTERN OREGON UNIVERSITY
MR. STERLING STEWART
MS. VENITA HAWKINS, IMMEDIATE PAST PRESIDENT OF THE KSU NATIONAL ALUMNI ASSOCIATION
(KSUNAA)
MR. RANDOLPH WILLIAMS, PRESIDENT OF THE KSU K-CLUB
MS. KIMBERLEY REED-THOMPSON, IMMEDIATE VP OF THE KSUNAA
MR. ROBERT GRIFFIN, KSU MUSIC DEPARTMENT
MS. KEMBA COFIELD
MR. KOLOMO BAILEY
DR. VERNELL BENNETT, FORMER K-RETTE COORDINATOR
DRS. VIVIAN AND DOWELL TAYLOR OF JACKSON STATE UNIVERSITY
MS. KEELIA BROWN OF HBCU DANCE CORP
ALL OF THE PHOTOGRAPHERS AND VIDEOGRAPHERS WHO PROMOTE HBCU MARCHING
BANDS...SOMETIMES YOU DO NOT RECEIVE YOUR JUST DUE IN THIS FIELD OF MEDIA
UCHE AND WILL...THOROBREDS FOREVER. THANKS FOR YOUR SACRIFICES PROMOTING THE MIGHTY
MARCHING THOROBREDS
THE ALUMNI K-RETTES. THANKYOU FOR YOUR SUPPORT AND LOVE OVER THE YEARS.
MS. SHELBY PATRICE JENKINS...THANK YOU FOR YOUR LOVE AND PATRONAGE.
THE KSU THOROBREDS FAMILY

MOSTLY, I WANT TO THANK GOD, HIS SON JESUS, AND MY FAMILIES OF THE RICES AND DUNNS